OUR STORY

OUR STORY
A WORLD WAR II SURVIVAL AND MIGRATION TO AMERICA

Ilse Adler

with editing by
John Steve Adler

MCP - MAITLAND, FL

Mill City Press, Inc.
2301 Lucien Way #415
Maitland, FL 32751
407·339·4217
www.millcitypublishing.com

ISBN-13: 978-1-63505-581-8
LCCN: 2017900918

Edited by
John Steve Adler, Lillian nee Adler Ostendorf, Robert Adler

Translated by
Ilse Adler, Susie nee Goetz Fischman

Printed in the United States of America

CONTENTS

INTRODUCTION

Ilse Adler began writing about the life events in the Adler family, from her early courtship by Henry to their travels during the late 1970s and continuing into the 1990s, after their retirement. This book began as a first-person account by Ilse.

During the 1990s, Ilse asked Steve, her oldest son, to assist in editing the story, which had several chronological chapters. The story has been modified and edited from first person by Ilse to third person by Steve. Over the Adler years that followed Henry and Ilse's retirement, Steve made oral history tapes with Ilse and Henry. The content of these tapes, in concert with passports and other saved documents, has been used to determine certain event dates, including international travel. Thanks to Lillian Ostendorf Adler, Bob Adler, and Shelley Jo Schaub for their additions, comments, and recommendations.

HENRY AND ILSE IN VIENNA, AUSTRIA

Henry Adler and Ilse Götz (Goetz) were born and raised in Vienna, Austria, during the rule of Emperor Franz Josef of the Habsburg dynasty.

Henry was born September 4, 1907, and Ilse was born January 31, 1913.

Both Henry's and Ilse's parents' marriages had been arranged, as was customary in those days. Both sets of parents were middle class. Henry's father owned a number of coffeehouses, and, soon after World War I, Ilse's parents also owned a coffeehouse/restaurant in a Viennese park.

Ilse's father, Julius Götz (Goetz), originally was employed by the state-owned railway. Julius had been a counsel, and this provided him a pension on retirement. In addition, over objections by some family members, Julius bought a derailed boxcar of salt. This was extremely useful during the Depression, when inflation made bartering important. Julius was able to trade the salt for food and other goods while working for the railway.

ILSE AND HENRY MEET

Henry and Ilse first met in 1934, when Henry came to collect Ilse's father's membership dues for an organization of coffeehouse and restaurant owners.

Ilse said she fell in love with this handsome fellow with "the kissable lips" then and there. Ilse met Henry socially later that year, when cousins invited her to join their ping-pong club. From then on, Henry and Ilse's courtship developed—slowly.

THEIR FAMILY BACKGROUND

Ilse's father, Julius Goetz was born on May 21, 1879, in the small town of Puklice in Moravia. Julius's father, Leopold, was a schoolteacher, and his mother, Philippine Wessely, was a homemaker. Julius was one of ten siblings. He earned a juris doctor degree at the University of Vienna. Julius, however, never practiced private law. He became a civil servant, working for the state-owned railway.

Ilse's mother, Belcza Acht, was born March 31, 1886, in Temesvar (Timisoara), Hungary, the youngest of eight siblings. Belcza had studied to become an opera singer, but her career was interrupted by rheumatoid arthritis. Belcza had a stiff right wrist and a crooked and stiff left index finger. This did not stop Belcza from playing the piano. Belcza often sang in what Ilse called a glorious mezzo-soprano voice.

Ilse's parents were married in 1910 in Vienna, Austria. They lived at 60 Nussdorfer Strasse. *Note 1* Both Ilse's parents were musically talented. Her father, Julius, played the violin, and Ilse learned to play the piano. They often played music together. This was how Ilse became fond of music, especially the classics.

Ilse had a sister, Suzanne (whom we all called Susie). Susie was born in Vienna on June 28, 1921. She lived in Traverse City, Michigan, most of her life. In December 1993, Susie suffered a stroke that partially paralyzed her. In July 1994, another stroke put her in a coma. Susie died July 19, 1994, and was buried July 21, 1996. *Note 2*

ILSE'S GRANDPARENTS

Ilse's paternal grandmother was a Wessely. Ilse's second cousin Esther (Annie) Wulasky was born a Wessely. Ilse learned that the Wesselys had been Catholic in the thirteenth or fourteenth century in Bohemia and had converted to Hussites. Esther learned this from her grandchildren living in Beer Sheva, Israel, who had studied their family's genealogy. The Catholics fought the Hussites for a decade, and the Hussites lost. The Hussites were persecuted, and Jan Hus was burned at the stake. Ilse pointed out, "As you can see, religious persecution is in our genes." The Wesselys refused to return to Catholicism and chose to convert to Judaism instead.

HENRY'S FAMILY

Henry's family lived at 51 Neulerchenfelder Strasse. *Note 3* His father, Sigmund Adler, was born April 18, 1870, in Mattersdorf (now Mattersburg), Austria. Sigmund was one of twenty-on children. Henry's grandfather was Heinrich Adler, who was a cobbler in the Ghetto. Henry's grandmother's name was Nettie. Nettie's maiden name is unknown. Nettie lived with her son Sigmund Adler until her death. (The date of her death is unknown.)

Henry's mother, Jeannette (née Austerlitz) was born in Bielitz on February 2, 1867. She died on October 16, 1938, in Vienna. Jeannette lived into her late seventies. Henry's father died on March 21, 1944, in Theresienstadt, a concentration camp. Henry's parents were married in Vienna sometime around 1900.

Henry had two older brothers, Maximilian and Leopold. The Adler family lived at 51 Neulerchenfelder Strasse in Vienna.

Maximilian and Leopold perished in the Holocaust (date and place unknown, somewhere in Poland). Ilse's parents also perished in the Holocaust, most likely in Auschwitz, in 1944.

ILSE AND EDUCATION

According to Ilse, she was a precocious child. Before she started school in Vienna, she had learned to read using the words and letters on the streetcars.

Once, while on a vacation, she wanted to write a letter to her father. She asked her mother to help her with the words and letters she did not know. Later, when she began school, she could already read her schoolbooks.

Ilse said that all through school she was bored. She felt awkward listening to classmates who stumbled through words, letter by letter, losing all meaning of what they were reading. In those days, there were no gifted-child advancement classes that Ilse could take.

Ilse was a fast learner; she grasped concepts and meanings quickly. Ilse often dawdled over her homework with its meaningless repetitiveness. Like many Adlers, Ilse felt her grades were never commensurate with her abilities. She was often scolded for inattentiveness, as she had her nose in a book, reading a story.

Grade school was five years. While in grade school, Ilse met Hedda Frucht and her brother, Karl. They became good friends. They adored their grade school teacher, Bertha Falk.

In their fifth year, they had two interesting experiences. The first was a visit by psychologists (Ilse later presumed), who asked the kids to tell about their dreams. Ilse recalled vividly the dream that she related to them—she dreamed that the world was coming to an end. One half of the globe was turned inside out, and she was watching it from somewhere in space.

The second experience was that some people came and introduced what she thought, in retrospect, was "project teaching." The students were given the task of preparing for an outing. They were told to list items and their prices to buy for lunch and snacks. They were told also to select and price railroad tickets and then figure out the total cost of the field trip.

Ilse was enrolled in a private girls' *Realgymnasium*. She entered classes late due to illness. Her mother had taken her to Merano, Italy, where Ilse convalesced from pneumonia contracted during the summer.

The Realgymnasium was an eight-year school. The students were taught seven years of Latin, physics, chemistry, biology, and higher mathematics. The students also were taught history, geography, and German literature. In the last three years, Ilse chose English as her foreign language rather than French. She already had seven years of private lessons in French. When Ilse graduated, she had the equivalent of a junior college education.

In the fall of 1934, Ilse matriculated to the University of Vienna Medical School. She was not able to finish, however, due to the Nazi activities in Vienna.

HENRY AND EDUCATION

Henry went to grade school in various districts of Vienna, as his family often moved. Henry told Ilse that he cut classes frequently because he preferred to play soccer and other games with his friends.

Henry was very bright. He made it into secondary school and then into business school. At age seventeen, Henry got his first job in a bank and later moved to another bank. Henry had to leave work, however, when he became ill. He was sent to recover in Yugoslavia for six weeks by his health insurance. When Henry returned, his father sent him to Berlin to work, where Henry held a variety of jobs. Henry, who was a good ballroom dancer, confided to Steve that he spent many evenings escorting women while in Berlin.

When Henry returned to Vienna, he got a job with the Association of the Restaurant and Coffeehouse Owners. This was his work when he met Ilse. In 1934, Henry lost this job due to the political changes in Austria. After that, he worked in two hotels and had various other jobs until their emigration.

HENRY AND ILSE'S COURTSHIP

Their courtship began slowly at a ping-pong club. Henry was a bashful beau. At first, Henry would join a group to walk Ilse home. Later, when it was raining, he would take her home by taxi. Henry was employed then at the same office as Ilse's cousin.

Refreshments were sold at the ping-pong club, and when Ilse bought a cup of coffee, Henry would buy some sweets and sit down at her table. Without a word, he would push them over to her, and they would have a conversation of sorts. However, he would usually address Ilse in the formal way as "Fraulein."

When Ilse's birthday rolled around, she had a party, and, among others, she invited "Mr. Adler." Henry brought her an expensive present, a silver compact with her name engraved on it. (Ilse brought it to America, but it eventually was lost.) They started dating. Henry took her to movies and theater shows, always buying expensive tickets. They went dancing, and as they eventually became closer, Henry started to use the familiar and more intimate German "you."

They became officially engaged. Henry was introduced to the many members of Ilse's parents' family and relatives. They visited back and forth between their parents' homes. Ilse continued with her study of medicine, and Henry had a good job. They continued to date. Henry took her on many excursions into the Vienna Woods.

In February 1934, Henry lost his job. There was a political coup by the Fascist "Home Guard," which resulted in the murder of Chancellor Engelbert Dollfuss. This caused a civil war, in which the Fascists bombed the Karl Marx Hof. The Social Democrats, with whom Henry was involved, lost their positions.

The Nazi Party was declared illegal and went underground. The Nazi Party, however, as we found out later, continued strong. Ilse's parents' business was bombed, and that caused the end of her study at the University of Vienna. While at the university, Ilse had been caught up in student riots, in which a friend of her cousin had been killed.

Later that summer, Henry got a job running two hotels in the Salzkammergut. One was in Bad Ischl and the other in St. Gilgen. Ilse went there to visit him. At the end of the season, they returned to Vienna, where they both worked in her parents' business. Ilse became a partner of the bridge club director. The bridge club continued during that winter in a big coffeehouse. Henry also worked with them in the bridge club. Some of the time, Henry helped out in his father's coffeehouse. The outlook for employment was bleak, to say the least.

As they heard about the anti-Semitic excesses in Germany and Hitler's intention to annex Austria, it created a hopeless out-look for their life in Vienna. They agreed on two things: they had to emigrate, and they had a better chance of working for better times together, rather than separately.

HENRY AND ILSE'S MARRIAGE

They persuaded their parents to help them get married. They were married May 21, 1935, in the central synagogue in Vienna. *Note 4*

After a brief honeymoon, they lived in furnished rooms and continued their precarious lives in a now very dangerous Vienna.

In December 1937, Ilse became pregnant. Her gynecologist recommended that Ilse register at the largest lying-in hospital of Vienna. This was because he would be leaving Vienna but said that she would have the best prenatal care there. The hospital received her medical history and gave her papers to present for admission when time came to give birth. This prearrangement allowed her admission without further question. It turned out to be very good in many respects that Ilse followed his advice.

In February 1938, Ilse was ordered to bed because she started to spot. While she was in bed, she heard on the radio that Chancellor Schuschnigg had gone to Berchdesgaden to plead with Hitler to desist in his intention to annex Austria. Ilse later heard that Hitler had thrown one of his famous tantrums and screamed at Schuschnigg.

The chancellor announced that he would call a plebiscite for March 13, 1938, to let the Austrians decide for themselves. This was announced in the papers and on radio and on billboards, as well as on the pavement of many streets. It never came to pass because on March 11, 1938, the Nazis marched across the border. Ilse felt that the invasion was abetted by Schuschnigg's pleas to the Austrians to not resist annexation by Hitler.

Henry and Ilse had worked in her parents' business, the café in the Waehringer Park. During that winter, they worked in another coffee house near her parents' home.

Later that year (1938), they were forced to give up their rented room. They moved in with her parents at Nussdorfer Strasse 60.

The place where they worked was about three blocks away from Nussdorfer Strasse 60. The evening of March 11, 1938, was cold, and on the way home, they were very depressed. They noticed a few rowdies walking behind them. Ilse hung on tightly to Henry's arm. They did not turn around and did not walk faster. When they came to the entrance of the house and went in, the rowdies came in behind them. They still did not turn around. As they crossed the few steps to the glass door, where their stairway began, the rowdies turned around and left. Henry and Ilse had expected to get beaten up or worse. They were relieved to reach the floor where they lived unscathed.

The next day, Ilse called Henry's brothers to ask them to go to every consulate and embassy to find out to where they could immigrate. Thus, Henry and Ilse were registered at the

American embassy and received a low number (a good position) on the list of applicants.

A few days after the *Anschluss,* two new Nazi Party members came to the apartment and told them they had to evacuate it. Ilse remembered clearly how her father stood there with his arms across his chest and said, "I won't go." Ilse fully expected that one or both of these men would slap her father around— or worse. In the meantime, her mother asked one of them to accompany her through the apartment. The apartment was arranged so a person could walk in a circle while going from one room to the next and then come back to the starting point. While doing this, she quietly explained to the man that there were actually two families living in this place and that Ilse was expecting. When they rejoined Ilse, her father and the other man in the entry hall, the man said to the other, "Let's go," and they left them alone.

The next day some storm troopers came to the door and demanded that Ilse's father come to scrub the plebiscite announcements off the streets. However, Ilse's sister, Susie, volunteered to go instead, which she did.

A short while later, Susie was brought back by two former waitresses from their business. Susie explained what had happened—the Nazis had fetched people from various nearby apartment houses, among them a friend of the family. These were well-dressed people, and it was cold. They wore coats, hats, and gloves. The Nazis insisted that they bring pails, soap, and brushes, and regardless of their good clothes, they made the people get down on their knees and scrub. When an elderly man did not scrub as fast as they wanted him to do, one of the Nazis hit him on the head with the butt of his rifle. That is when Susie fainted. The waitresses, who were in the crowd that had gathered to watch, brought her home. The crowd had been cheering on the Nazis and jeering at the abused Jews. Ilse often stated that this was only one of the many instances where the Austrians showed their true colors.

Henry and Ilse realized that they could not stay in the Third Reich. They and many others tried to get passports and all the necessary papers to emigrate. This turn of events, oddly, provided Henry with an opportunity to earn some money. Henry worked as a stand-in for people who were too scared to wait in line for papers themselves.

Ilse was also able to earn some money selling soaps, wash powders, and cosmetics, which she got on consignment from a druggist they knew. Ilse took two heavy shopping bags full of materials, at first to people she knew and then, with their recommendations, to others. This involved climbing many flights of stairs with her heavy load. Ilse said this probably helped to keep her in good shape while she was pregnant. In addition, she could contribute money to her parents' household.

Ilse's sister, Susie, was working then as a secretary at the Central Jewish Congregational Office. As far as living expenses were concerned, they could manage, but nobody was safe anywhere from Nazi attacks. None of them knew, when leaving their houses, whether they would return. They lived though this most stressful and upsetting time, but worse was yet to come.

Ilse continued her monthly visits to the hospital. When many of their friends emigrated, they gave Henry and Ilse all sorts of baby things—a crib, a changing table, bathtubs, and a most fanciful layette, all for the baby they were expecting.

One morning Ilse had a checkup and the doctor said, "Most any time now." Later that day, they received a gorgeous armoire with cut-glass doors. Ilse was watching the movers put it together, and one of the men bumped into one of the glass doors. Ilse jumped up to catch the door, fearing the glass would break. Later that same afternoon, they had coffee, and Henry left for one of his jobs. As Ilse helped her mother clear the table, her water broke—yes, the baby was on the way.

JOHANN STEFAN (JOHN STEVE) ADLER IS BORN

I lse's doctor ordered her into the hospital. *Note 5* Her father took her there, and she was admitted without any questions. John Steve was born at 8:30 p.m., August 23, 1938. Afterward, Ilse had to wait over an hour before being taken back to her room. Henry had been waiting in the corridor to see her, to make sure she was all right.

There were two other Jewish women in the birthing unit. The Jewish women, including Ilse, had been put in the isolation ward. Thus, they each had a private room instead of being put in the eighteen-bed ward. Of course, this was so as not to contaminate the pure Aryan mothers!

Their baby boy was named Johann Stefan. At that time, they did not know where they would wind up in the world and felt that this name would be easily translated in most languages. Thus, he became John Steve when they came to the USA. He was a great joy and solace to them all in the hard and difficult times that followed.

Two weeks after their son was born, mother and baby were discharged from the hospital. Ilse received a pink slip that certified that they had been discharged. The slip was properly stamped and signed. This pink piece of paper played a very important part in their subsequent preparations to emigrate.

The first few weeks after returning to her parents' home were spent in blissful happiness. They used the many fancy gifts items for the new baby, among them a deep English perambulator received from a former girlfriend prior to her departure for the USA.

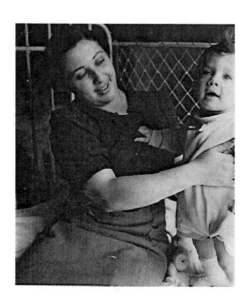

They took their new son to his paternal grandparents. There, Henry's mother, Jeanette, was deep in her grieving over her firstborn son, Maximillian. Max had been sent to KZ (concentration camp) Buchenwald after the Nazi takeover in Austria. Jeanette suffered a series of strokes. She died on October 16, 1938. She was buried in Vienna's Zentral Friedhof in a crypt, together with a sister and a brother-in-law.

[In 1990, Ilse came to Vienna with her daughter, Lillian, and sister, Susie. While there, they tried to find Henry's mother's grave but were unable to do so. **Note 6**]

After Henry's mother's funeral, they had a six-week respite, and then the sky fell: *Kristallnacht!*

Henry was out on one of his errands as a stand-in for other prospective emigrants. He was arrested inside the grounds of the English embassy. He had left home at 9:00 p.m. Ilse had the distinct feeling that she would not see him for a long time. Of course, at that moment all she knew was that he had not returned home. During the night, Ilse had taken the baby into her bed. He was securely bundled in a swaddling quilt, so she could not roll onto him and suffocate him. The baby next to her gave her solace, and she went back to sleep. Ilse was dreaming that she was in a huge railway station hall, when the telephone rang and woke her. The telephone call was from an inner-city policeman to come to the station.

Ilse and her father went to the station. There, as Henry embraced Ilse's father, he slipped the papers from the "errand" into her father's pocket. Later that same day, they learned that the Nazis had arrested every Jewish man they could find.

During the following two weeks, Ilse did not know whether Henry was dead or alive. Ilse and her parents finally received a letter from him. Henry was in the concentration camp Dachau.

At that time, everyone "knew" that no one ever returned from a concentration camp.

Ilse continued as best she could to prepare for their emigration. In early December, a registered letter arrived addressed to Henry, and the mailman did not let Ilse sign for it; he sent it on to Dachau. Ilse had seen that it was from Detroit and immediately sent a cablegram to her cousin Ellie in Detroit, stating, "Henry is by Max," who also was in a concentration camp, and asked Ellie to send copies of the affidavit. New copies were sent and included Susie's name.

Unfortunately, long afterward, they found out that the person who gave the affidavit had overdrawn his resources, and these affidavits were worthless. So their waiting for new affidavits started all over again.

During these trying times, Ilse's parents were incredibly wonderful and gave her moral, emotional, and material support. They had no income other than Susie's earnings—she worked as a secretary at the Jewish Congregational Office. Their father's small pension was just enough to pay the rent, so they gradually "ate up" many possessions, including their piano, her mother's jewelry, their Persian rugs, and her parents' fur coats.

Ilse's parents did not complain. At times, Ilse would sit at the table and seem unable to eat. Her parents told her that she needed to conserve her strength to care for the baby. They urged her to continue every effort to ready the required papers for their emigration.

Then, suddenly, Vienna was abuzz with rumors that various people had been released from Dachau upon proving that he could leave the German Reich. What to do? What to do? The only place on the face of the earth where one could go without a visa, permit, or affidavit of support was Shanghai, China. That cost much money, which they did not have.

Ilse then telephoned a cousin in Belgrade and begged her to book passage for Henry to China. The cousin sent her a telegram, stating that passage had been booked on a particular line for Henry Adler to go to Shanghai. Ilse went to the Gestapo with this telegram, and two weeks later, Henry was released.

Ilse went to the Westbahnhof several days in a row, and on February 24, 1939, she finally saw Henry coming toward her. Her heart felt like it was ballooning in her chest. Henry, however, did not seem to see her; he walked like in a trance. At the station, Henry waited for her outside a telephone booth while she called her parents to tell them that he was back. They took a streetcar home. Henry neither looked at her nor spoke. He was like a zombie.

It took several days for Henry to cope with his return. Henry told them that prisoners had been warned not to talk about the camp.

When Henry was in Dachau, he wrote several letters to Ilse, and she brought them all to the United States when they emigrated.

In 1984–85, when Henry and Ilse were in Israel, they turned over the letters and other materials to Yad Vashem, the Israeli Holocaust Memorial. They kept photocopies and considered adding them to this story, but the letters, as well as the copies of her replies, are in German and not translated, so they are not included.

It took several years—long after coming to the USA—before Henry could relate some of his experiences, many of which he was never able to tell.

A group of eighth graders and their teacher came to the house in Traverse City to interview Henry and Ilse about the Holocaust. When one of the girls asked Henry how it felt to be forced to do things, he told how he was punished for dropping a paint-brush in freezing weather. He was hung by his hands from a tree for about fifteen minutes. He also told about being beaten at Gestapo headquarters for refusing to sign a false confession to *Rassenschande* (having intercourse with an Aryan woman). He was hit on the head until he passed out and later woke up in his cell. He also described how, later, he and the other prisoners were taken to Munich in the infamous "Light Train" (so named because the prisoners were forced to sit with their hands on their knees, staring into the light bulbs overhead). When Henry asked to go to the toilet, he was severely beaten. When the train arrived in Munich, Henry, together with other prisoners, were forced to carry out the bodies of the prisoners who had died on the train. Henry recognized one boy only by a ring on his finger.

On the morning after they arrived at Dachau (with the infamous inscription over the gate, "Arbeit Macht Frei"), the prisoners were assembled in the square for roll call. Henry heard his brother Leopold's name called—Leopold was also there in Dachau. (He also eventually was released from Dachau.)

Among the many atrocities Henry witnessed was that no one was allowed to assist someone who had fallen, and as a result, many died where they fell. When Henry returned to the barracks, he found several who had hanged themselves. Henry often said it was a miracle in itself to survive this and all the atrocities that dehumanized and demeaned the prisoners.

In Vienna, Henry had to report to the police at intervals. After a few weeks, he was told to report to the Gestapo. They told him that if he was not out of Vienna within forty-eight hours, he would be sent back to the concentration camp. Henry went to the Jewish Central Congregational Office and asked for help. The director tried to dismiss Henry by telling him that there were hundreds like him, and they could not help. Henry got angry and, after a few choice words, stalked out of the office. The director came after him and suggested that he try the Palestine agency in an office across from his. When Henry went in there, the official asked him whether he still was a Jew. When Henry said yes, the man picked up the telephone and called the Gestapo. The man said he had Henry Adler, recently released from Dachau, in his office and that he could use him at the newly established Hachschera camp at the estate of Mautner-Markhoff (an estate owned by a Jew that had been confiscated). The Gestapo gave permission, and Henry's life was saved for the moment.

Henry went to the estate, which was a few hours by train from Vienna. There, Henry found a group of teenage Jewish boys and girls who were being trained in agriculture for the purpose of immigrating to Palestine. They were housed in the horse stables, while the manager from the Gestapo was living in the mansion. Happy to be there, Henry befriended the Gestapo manager and went drinking with him in the local tavern. Henry partially recuperated from the stresses of his stay at the concentration camp.

Meanwhile, Ilse continued with preparations for their emigration.

Years later, when Henry finally began to speak of his experiences, he said that on the day of his arrest, he found himself in the same cell as one of the men for whom Henry had stood in line at the English embassy. This man said that he would be released after he made a telephone call. Henry related the following story about that man:

> During the time when the Nazis were outlawed in Austria, this man was in a hotel in Graz. In the middle of the night someone knocked on his door and begged him to let him hide because somebody was after him. He identified himself as Herman Goering. Later, Goering told him if he ever was arrested to call a certain telephone number, and he would be released.

This call was made on the day after the Kristallnacht. The man also told Henry that he would help Ilse with money, which he later did.

On January 23, 1939, Ilse went to secure a most important document for their emigration. This was a statement that they did not owe any taxes (*die Steuerunbedenklichkeit Erklaerung*). Ilse went to the Rothschild Palace in the Prinz Eugen Strasse (the Nazis picked their official locations satanically). There, she found people lined up, four abreast, clear around the block. They told her that they sometimes had to return the next day to get in. Ilse was disheartened. She could not stay away from home longer than three hours since she was still nursing her son. What should she do? Ilse had an inspiration. She went up to the door where a young SA (German army) man stood. She took out the pink hospital release slip with its official-looking stamps. She asked this young man (who appeared to be about sixteen or seventeen) whether he could do something for her since she had an infant at home who had to be nursed every three hours.

He blushed and stammered, "Wait here." He then left and shortly came back with an SS man (storm trooper, black uniform, death head and crossbones on his cap). The SS man looked at the release slip, scratched his head, and told her, "Come along." The SS man was Viennese and about Ilse's age. He told her that he too had an infant son and escorted her through the huge rooms where all the green-felt-covered tables stood. There, she got one stamp after the other on her papers—a miracle. The whole procedure took less than half an hour. The SS man even told her his name and pulled a photo from his wallet, a picture of his baby. Ilse had expected to be slapped or beaten up or arrested. Happily, she ended up with this precious document back at home. This was one of the many instances when their son's birth helped with their emigration.

Ilse received a call on June 2, 1939, to come to the American embassy for a physical examination, which was needed prior to receiving emigration papers for travel to America. Ilse then sent Henry a postcard with this information.

Earlier, the leader of the Hachschera camp had invited Henry to travel with their group to Palestine. Henry would have had a certificate, which would have made his immigration legal. Henry, however, declined because there were no certificates for Ilse and their son. Upon receiving the American embassy information from Ilse, Henry went to the Gestapo manager and asked him how he could return to Vienna.

A few weeks earlier, the Gestapo manager announced that Adolf Eichmann was coming to inspect the camp. When Eichmann was there, he insulted Henry with a few choice epithets, as was the usual way to deal with a former concentration camp inmate. Henry had learned in the concentration camp, Dachau, not to react or answer, so he was not physically accosted. The camp passed inspection without incident. Henry was now in good standing with the Gestapo manager.

The Gestapo manager told Henry to fill a knapsack with a few chickens and fresh eggs, and he gave Henry the money for train fare.

When Henry arrived in Vienna, he looked great—suntanned and with a curly new growth of hair (in the concentration camp, the men were shorn).

On the day of their physical examination at the American embassy, Ilse was very nervous, and a pimple like skin eruption broke out on her face. The doctor asked what that was, and she explained that she often broke out when she was nervous. Henry's and Ilse's examinations were satisfactory, and they were told they could get their papers at the end of the week. The skin eruption on her face later turned out to be impetigo. Ilse went to be treated at the only hospital available to Jews. She had to be extremely careful so that her son's nursing would not be affected. Due to this infection, Ilse did not even kiss her mother good-bye when they were ready to leave.

LEAVING VIENNA

Their fathers and Henry's brothers went with them to the train station. This was the last time Henry and Ilse saw any of them alive. After Henry and Ilse left Vienna, Leopold and his brother Maximillian were shipped to Poland as laborers, never to be heard from again.

When the people in their train compartment realized that they were Jews, they complained loudly and moved to another compartment. Thus, Henry and Ilse had the entire compartment to themselves. They were able to stretch out and lie down for the thirty-six-hour trip to the Holland border.

They stopped at Emmerich, on the German side of the border. The customs agents were SA (German soldiers). All the refugees, including Ilse, Henry, and the baby, were ordered off the train. The customs agents took their time with examining the luggage, including examining shoe cream, soap, and toothpaste for the possible smuggling of diamonds or other valuables.

Ilse changed the baby. When Henry tried to throw the diaper in the trash, he was jumped by an SA, who yelled, "What are you throwing away?". Henry, still very afraid of any German uniform, froze and held the diaper open under the guy's nose (and Ilse was always sorry that it was only wet!).

Meanwhile, the train had pulled away. Henry asked the station agent when the next train would come. He told him, "Not for twenty-four hours." So Henry asked what they could do, as they were not allowed into the village. Also, they had only the monetary equivalent of twelve dollars—the Nazis allowed them to take only four dollars per person. The station agent said that in a few minutes the *Orient Express* would come through to take on mail, water, and the customs agents. He told Henry to get their stuff together and get on that train quickly, which they did. The train had first- and second-class cars only, so they had to pay five dollars. They were glad to finally be out of Germany (and Austria).

When they arrived in Rotterdam late that night, they stood on the platform, trying to decide what to do. Soon, a lady came along, calling out "Adlers!" It turned out that she had been looking for them on every arriving train. The lady took them in a waiting limousine to the Jewish agency office. There, they were asked what kind of accommodations they wanted— whether they wanted to go to a hotel, a private room, or a boarding house. They asked for the boarding house and were taken to a kosher pension. The landlady arranged for a crib to be brought to their room. She offered to let Ilse fix whatever her son needed.

Henry was asked to come to the Jewish agency office. He was handed twenty gilders, with the suggestion to buy flowers for Ilse and cigarettes for himself. When they came to the open-air market, they were stunned by the abundance of foods, flowers, and dry goods.

In Vienna, all food stuffs had become scarce. In the Vienna butcher's window, instead of sausages and hams, there were flowering plants. In Vienna, the grocer (where Ilse had shopped since she was a small child), making sure that she was unob-served, would sometimes give Ilse an orange or an apple under the counter "for the baby." There were severe penalties for aiding Jews.

At the market in Rotterdam, they saw tables piled high with loaves of bread and lots of butter. At this time in Germany, Goebbels proclaimed in his notorious speech that the German people had to choose between butter and cannons.

They had to wait a week for their boat, the *Statendam*, to leave. They took long walks on the wharf. There, they learned to enjoy specialties like freshly caught herring fillets, which were offered with salt and crackers out of pushcarts similar to an ice cream vendor's cart.

Their landlady had voiced her fears about the Germans, who were only half an hour away. As it turned out, her fears were well founded. During the war, Rotterdam was bombed to the ground by the Germans.

SAILING TO THE UNITED STATES

Finally, on July 24, 1939, they boarded the ship to the USA. They had a cabin with four bunks, way down in the bottom of the boat. However, one lower bunk was removed to make room for a crib. They had their own private cabin. Henry gave the steward his last five dollars as a tip, and they were treated very well. Anything they wanted or needed for the baby was provided. Steve was eleven months old when they crossed the Atlantic Ocean.

Henry and Ilse were two of the few passengers who did not get seasick, and they were treated with an abundance of food in the beautiful but mostly empty dining room. The only other passenger in the dining room, who later joined them, was an American teacher, returning home.

The crossing took nine days. They had calm seas except for one night when it stormed. Ilse often went up on the highest deck, enjoying the wind blowing through her hair. On some evenings they went up to the salon, where other refugees from Vienna gathered. One of them was Bert Silving, a well-known radio personality. He played the piano. They all sang in nostalgic Vienna Lieder and cried about having to leave Vienna. This angered Henry, who was grateful to be out of the cauldron of Europe. The last Henry and Ilse had seen of Europe were searchlights stabbing the black sky, an eerie omen.

They arrived in New York Harbor on August 1, 1939. Ilse was in the cabin, changing the baby, as they came by the Statue of Liberty. They docked in Hoboken. It was a long drawn-out process to pass through the immigration officials' long tables. At first, they were not allowed off the boat until the Hebrew Immigration Aid Society (HIAS) vouched for them. They were not finished until 2:00 a.m. Ilse's cousins Anny and Karl Ross and another cousin Oscar Ultman, who had been waiting since the ship arrived, then assisted them through customs.

Henry had a typical experience that was funny in retrospect. He went to the bathroom. There, suddenly, an immigration official stuck his hand in Henry's pocket and pulled out an apple and an orange. He yelled at Henry that this was forbidden. Henry, who did not understand English, was frightened and upset. Ilse's cousin Oscar came to the rescue. He translated what the immigration official said about the fruit. They then went through customs smoothly. There, a huge New York policeman stood, telling them, "Take it easy, take it easy!"

They finally stepped off the boat on to dry land. Ilse was still rocking from the ship's motion. Henry had fifty-two cents left, which he spent on a Coke and a pack of cigarettes. Anny and Karli took them on the subway to Brighton Beach, Brooklyn. They had rented them a room in the same rooming house where they and some of Ilse's other cousins lived.

Henry, Ilse, and the baby had an attic room with one double bed but no crib. The baby slept between them and promptly fell out of bed but did not get hurt. They celebrated the baby's first birthday on the beach at Coney Island. Ilse had bought him a little playsuit in the dime store for ten cents.

It was a very hot August. Ilse quickly learned to walk the two blocks to the beach in her swimming suit. Ilse also went shopping in the grocery stores. The Brooklynites did not understand her "king's high English" (and she, conversely, could not understand them). However, she could read the labels and was able to shop.

Henry decided to find his first cousin Fritz Turk. Henry went to do this on the first day following his meeting at the HIAS agency office in Manhattan. Henry was asked to come to the HIAS office each day to review the family status. Having an address for Fritz on a piece of paper, Henry approached a policeman to ask for directions. Since Henry didn't understand or speak English, he showed the piece of paper to the policeman. When the policemen realized Henry did not understand English, he tried other languages. Luckily, he hit upon Yiddish. Henry then understood the policeman and, with new directions, started to walk across Central Park to Yorktown, where his cousin lived.

Henry was startled and somewhat frightened in that neighborhood. He thought he was back in Germany since there were German signs on the stores, Nazi flags all over the place, and Hitler's picture in the store windows. When Henry arrived at his cousin's, Fritz and his wife were at home. They treated him to some coffee and food. Later, his cousin Fritz picked up a lunch bucket and said he had to go to work. He asked Henry if he wanted a job. Henry answered yes, he did. Fritz said he probably could get him a job waiting tables where he worked. However, Fritz said he would have to greet the customers with "Heil Hitler." Henry replied with a few nasty expletives and then said, "No thank you." His cousin offered him a dollar to get back to Brooklyn. Henry refused, knowing he had a nickel in his pocket, which he used to return to Brooklyn.

Several years earlier, his cousin Fritz had returned to Vienna to find a girl to marry. He had flashed a roll of dollars, American style. He tried to give everyone the impression that he had become a rich American. Many years later, Henry and Ilse went to New York for a convention. Henry tried to find cousin Fritz again, but he wasn't there anymore.

Sometime after Steve's first birthday, he came down with a sore throat. Ilse and Henry called a physician, who treated Steve and prescribed medication. Henry asked him for a bill for reimbursement by the committee since they did not have money to pay. The doctor said that he would not be sending a bill.

After five weeks in New York without being able to find work, Henry went to meet again with the HIAS committee. There, he was told that the family was being sent to Detroit, where the person lived who had provided the affidavits of support. Two train tickets were provided: a coach ticket for Henry and a Pullman ticket for Ilse and the baby.

TRAVELING TO DETROIT

After boarding the train, Henry left to go to his seat in the coach car, but Ilse asked him to bring her a drink of water. He did not return for a long time, and she became worried about what had happened to him. Ilse, who was in a sleeping gown, got dressed, secured the baby in the bed, with the straps from the curtain, and went to the coach car. It was totally empty except for one lonely passenger: her husband. He sat there, green in the face, holding his hand. Ilse asked what had happened. He told her he had caught his left middle finger in the door and then had gone back to his seat. The conductor tried to help him, but there was a communications problem. The conductor had given him an aspirin and some water.

They were traveling on the Labor Day weekend, and this train went through Canada. The war in Europe had started on the third of September. Thus, they were told that they could not get off the train in Canada because they were considered enemy aliens.

When they arrived in Detroit, Ilse's cousin Ellie and her husband, Stefan, were there to pick them up. They took them to their home.

Three weeks after their arrival, Ilse had an accident. Her cousin lived on the second floor. Ilse fell down the stairs and broke her left wrist. Stefan, Ellie's husband, insisted that he should take her to their doctor, despite her explanation that she had to go to a hospital to get the arm set. Stefan, who had just learned to drive his stick shift car, was afraid to go on any through street. It was slow going, since Stefan had to stop at every corner. After his doctor verified that Ilse had to go to the hospital to get the arm set, they started out for the hospital. Stefan, however, did not know the way. He stopped, left Henry and Ilse standing in the street, and went home. A lady who was standing at the nearby bus stop suggested that they call the police. They did, and the police came and took them to the hospital. For Henry, this was another trial because he was still afraid of any uniformed person.

After several weeks in Detroit, the HIAS committee that provided Henry and Ilse the money that sustained them told them they had been unable to find suitable refugee support needed for them in Detroit. The committee said that there was a small Jewish congregation in northern Michigan, in Traverse City, which had pledged to take two refugee families for resettlement. Henry and Ilse accepted this pledged support and were soon leaving Detroit.

TRAVERSE CITY, MICHIGAN

It was October 1939, and Steve was thirteen months old when they arrived in Traverse City. They left Detroit at 10:00 a.m. by bus and arrived in Traverse City at 8:45 p.m. The bus had arrived early. At that time the bus station was downtown in the 100 block of East Front Street at the old post office. They got off the bus with their few belongings, including a small suitcase, a playpen, and a stroller for the baby. Ilse's left arm was in a cast, and the baby was in her right arm. In the arrival confusion, they forgot their briefcase on the bus. The brief-case contained their German passports with the "J" stamped on them, photos, letters, and a few other things. Later, they attempted to find it and get the lost briefcase back. The bus company checked for them, but they never got it back.

So there they stood on the sidewalk, feeling lost and forlorn. They were waiting to be met by members of the congregation. Finally, two cars drove up on the other side of the street. Some men got out and came toward them, asking if they were the Adlers. The group consisted of Sol Cavitch, the president of the congregation, Abe Moorstein, and two or three other people whose names Ilse didn't remember. They were taken to the Cavitches' home on Eleventh Street. This was also Sol's grocery store, and the Cavitch family lived upstairs. They were fed a late supper there and, after eating, answered many questions from Sol Cavitch and others. Ilse and Henry also spent some of the evening relating their story. Soon after this exchange, they were told that the congregation decided to have them live tem-porarily with the Moorsteins (Abe and Itke) at 875 East State

Street. The congregation agreed to pay their rent and provide money for groceries.

At the Moorsteins', they had a bedroom upstairs with a crib for the baby. They were permitted to use the kitchen. The bathroom they used was downstairs next to the kitchen.

The Moorsteins became very fond of the baby. Steve started to walk in the snow. There is a photo of him carrying a big ball on Rose Street near where the Moorsteins lived.

The Moorsteins were extremely nice people and were very good to the family. Henry and Ilse later learned that the Moorsteins had two sons in college, and, in the summer of 1938, they had lost a daughter. The members of the congregation told them they felt it would be good for them to be with the Moorsteins to help the couple cope with their loss. The Moorsteins treated them as if they were their children. They let them bring the baby's playpen down into the living room, and in the evenings they invited them to listen to the radio with them.

They had a terrific Philco radio console. They usually listened to WJR in Cincinnati. Some programs were *Jack Benny, Fred*

Allen, Burns and Allen, and the first quiz program, the *Sixty-Four Dollar Question.* The actor who portrayed Gildersleeve would say "Give the lady in the balcony a silver dollar" each time somebody knew an answer.

Henry, not knowing English, learned some English by listening to the radio. Ilse renewed and expanded her knowledge of English.

The Moorsteins had come from Russia, as had most of the members of the congregation. They kept a kosher house, but in spite of this, Mrs. Moorstein permitted Ilse to use her kitchen. Mrs. Moorstein spoke broken English. Itke was not illiterate; she could read and write Yiddish. Mr. Moorstein—Abe—got a Yiddish newspaper from New York, the *Forwards.* It was printed in Hebrew, and Ilse later learned to read some of the words.

Henry and Ilse were invited to dinner by practically every Jewish family in town, and they were always given some things to take home, like baked goods. They became members of the congregation and remained members for the rest of their days.

Henry's concern was to find work, but work was scarce in Traverse City. Henry and Ilse had arrived at the end of the summer season. Traverse City was primarily a summer resort town at that time.

Some of the members of the congregation who owned real estate hired Henry to do odd jobs, like painting and minor repairs. Later, a scrap-iron dealer named Ginsburg, who was from Detroit, hired Henry. Together with a motley crew of bums, transients, and hoboes, Henry worked at the dumping ground. There, they found cars that had been abandoned, burned off burnables, and loaded the metal skeletons on trucks. Mr. Moorstein took Henry to Montgomery Ward and bought him work clothing—coveralls, heavy work gloves, work shoes, a cap—and a lunch bucket for this job.

When Henry came home after the first day on the job, he was covered with soot and dirt from head to toe. He had to take a bath before they could sit down to eat. Mrs. Moorstein, the good soul, said that this was "clean dirt." That job didn't last very long. It was dangerous and because of his lack of English, Henry almost got killed. He happened to be in the way of one of the trucks when it started to move, and he couldn't understand the warning from one of his fellow workers. In addition, he didn't understand when they asked for specific tools.

In mid-December 1939, the Tru-Fit Trouser Company, owned by Sol Neiman (originally from Chicago) moved to Traverse City from Indiana. It was a non-union sweatshop. As was usual in those days when unionization was attempted, the factory was dismantled the night after the crew was dismissed and moved elsewhere. In this case, the machinery and goods were moved to Traverse City.

The members of the congregation were glad to have this opportunity to get Henry a steady job. But Sol Neiman, Abe Neiman's father, who was then the owner of the factory, balked when approached by the congregation because he didn't want to hire a "German Jew." Members of the congregation urged the Neimans to hire Henry, which they did, reluctantly. Sol Neiman hired Henry when the factory was set up. Henry started out sweeping floors and setting up machinery. He needed help because of his language difficulties, and the chief cutter of the factory helped him in Yiddish. He read the instructions on the boxes and other materials to Henry. Soon, Henry worked as a pants presser. Later, Ilse worked at the factory off and on.

Henry and Ilse learned later that some Jewish immigrants from Germany had been very arrogant and had claimed that everything was better were they had come from. This attitude had incensed prospective employers, and these immigrants earned themselves the title of *Chez-nous* (French for "among us").

43

When they first arrived in Traverse City, Henry took care of both the baby and Ilse. Because Ilse's arm was in a cast, she couldn't dress or do anything. Ilse gave Henry instructions for cooking and many other things.

After they were with the Moorsteins for about four months, the congregation decided that they should move into a house. To Henry and Ilse, this meant something grand. They didn't know or realize what a poor excuse for a house the congregation intended. Steve was seventeen months old in January 1940, when they moved to East Eighth Street.

The house at 1011 East Eighth Street had a half broken-down front porch without a railing. It was a two-story dwelling with an entryway, dining room, living room, bedroom, and kitchen on the ground floor. Upstairs were two bedrooms. One of the bedrooms was made into a "bathroom," with a toilet and a washbasin. Ilse was quite pregnant at that time and insisted that their landlord, Mr. Aaron, put in a bathtub. This made her the talk of the congregation—such nerve for a penniless immigrant to demand a bathtub. The house had no basement, only a crawl space. It had a space heater in the dining room and a small wood stove with a hot water heater in the kitchen. They were given all sorts of furniture by the various members of the congregation. The house also had a shed adjoining the kitchen, which was used to store coal. They also had a small icebox out in the shed. There was a medium-sized yard on the side of the house, where Ilse was able to hang laundry to dry.

Ilse's sister, Susie, came to America in February 1940. She was sent to Traverse City by the Jewish Joint Distribution Committee (JDC), who worked to get family members to live together. This happened in spite of the protestation of the congregation's busybody. This unnamed congregant gave them a dressing down for having the audacity to have Susie come to Traverse City.

Susie came to Traverse City two months before Henry and Ilse's daughter, Lillian, was born. Susie arrived just in time to help them. Susie tried to get a job but nothing worked out, so she helped around the house. They were too poor to have a telephone, but they had a very good neighbor across the street, Mrs. Blixt, who let them use her telephone from time to time. On the evening before Lillian was born, Mrs. Blixt told Susie that she would leave her key in her mailbox so that if Ilse went into labor in the middle of the night, Susie could come and use their telephone to call a taxi. Mrs. Blixt told Susie to tell the driver that this was an emergency. (Susie did not know at that time what "emergency" meant, but she did as she was told.) Lil's birth happened just that way.

Lillian Elizabeth was born April 27, 1940, in Traverse City, Michigan. She was born at the county hospital. The hospital was arranged so that Ilse was given a glassed-in sun porch for her room, which made it a private room. The nursing staff was fantastically nice, and the nurses were very good to her.

Ilse was well cared for there, but she and Henry were unable to pay their thirty-dollar hospital bill until several years later.

In the hospital, Ilse was always hungry, since it did not occur to her that she could have asked for more to eat. She simply did not dare to ask since she was still cowed by her recent experience of being considered a "non-person," and that was coupled with shyness at the time.

The morning after Lillian was born, Ilse and Susie sent a telegram to their parents. Later, they were very happy to receive a letter from their mother, telling them that she had known all along that Ilse had been pregnant and that she knew Ilse was going to have a girl!

The county hospital was six miles south of Traverse City, on Cass Road, so Ilse had few visitors. Henry could only come out to see them when a good soul gave him a ride. Ilse never got bored, though, and read every magazine available. Ilse discovered that despite her school studies of English, she knew much less than she had thought.

Steve was twenty months old when his sister, Lillian, was born. He loved her right away and called her his "strawberry blonde." After Lil's birth, the nurses came to visit them at home on Eighth Street. They took "Johnny" and Ilse out to the lighthouse park at the end of the peninsula. Lil grew up to be a pretty blonde, blue-eyed girl.

The heating system on East Eight Street was so poor that during the winter following Lil's birth, her hands were blue with the cold. They had to put mittens on her. They did not complain.

Steve developed pneumonia. Ilse had to take him to the hospital and leave him there. It is hard to decide for whom this was more traumatic—Steve or Ilse. Steve could only speak German and could not communicate with the nurses. They put him in diapers. He could not even ask for a drink of water. He recovered from the pneumonia, but Henry and Ilse were both wrecks by the time he was finally allowed to come home. It's a good thing that Steve does not remember this experience.

Lil was fourteen months old when she started to walk. Ilse and Henry were sitting in their yard, a few feet from each other, when all of a sudden she started to toddle from one foot to the other. It was very funny—her feet took her where they wanted to go. The following Sunday, everyone dressed up and went visiting. Henry and Ilse each held one of Lil's hands, and they walked on Washington Street toward the houses of people they knew. Soon, of course, Daddy had to carry her, while big brother walked. In those days, it was easy for them to walk all across town.

That year they attended their first cherry festival. Ilse took the children and walked downtown—Lil in her baby buggy and "Johnny" alongside. Ilse even had a photo taken by a street photographer.

Susie tried for a number of jobs without success. Henry and Ilse arranged for Susie to move to Chicago to find work. Susie was also trying to find someone to provide an affidavit for their parents. Susie did not succeed. By the end of the year, she had become ill. She was in a hospital, without money and despondent. Henry and Ilse helped Susie return to Traverse City. Ilse went to work in the garment factory, Tru-Fit Trousers, while Susie kept house for them and took care of the children.

In the middle of 1941, Henry felt that he was earning sufficiently so that they could declare their independence from the congregation. Ilse still remembers the price of groceries in those days. Butter was twenty-eight cents a pound, eggs were ten cents a dozen, and coffee was thirty-seven cents for three pounds.

In 1942, when Henry and Ilse were both working at Tru-Fit Trousers, they were making about one dollar an hour. Thinking that this was a lot of money, they bought a 1937 Ford from Abe Moorstein for two hundred dollars. Later, the 1937 Ford was traded in on a 1934 Chevrolet, which they called "Lulabelle." (Henry called it a tank.)

THE HOUSE AT 223 GARFIELD AVENUE

After their daughter, Lil, was born, they still lived in that awful, inadequate "shack" on Eighth Street. They decided to look for a better place to live. The following summer of 1943, they found a house and moved to 223 Garfield. They were able to rent the downstairs rooms for the same amount they had paid to Mr. Aaron for the house on East Eighth Street.

The house, its yard, barn and garden at 223 Garfield Avenue, sat on almost an acre of land (the entire property was about three acres), had much more room. It had a parlor that they converted into the children's bedroom. It had a large living room, a dining room, a kitchen, a bathroom, and a bedroom, all on one floor. It also had a large screened-in porch off the dining room, a small anteroom, and a front porch. In the back of the kitchen was a large shed where they put their icebox and washing machine—an antique Maytag with a copper kettle and three bells to agitate the laundry. (Later, Ilse often wished they had kept it!)

There also was a large barn, which was supposed to serve as a garage. At the time they moved in, the barn was rented to a fellow who used it to store paper and other things. Later on, with the help of a friend, they built a chicken coop inside, where they raised chickens from baby chicks. Next to the barn and behind the house was a large field, which stretched up to the fairgrounds (now the Civic Center). On the right side of the field was a strawberry patch, in which asparagus also grew. They were delighted to have space for a "victory garden."

Members of the congregation tried to discourage this garden idea, since the ground was sandy and nothing had grown there for years. They tried anyway. They grew corn and beans quite successfully. They also had a crop of cucumbers, which Ilse made into pickles and was able to sell and then buy Henry a sweater. They also dug up part of the lawn in the back for an additional smaller garden. There, they grew tomatoes, lettuce, radishes, kohlrabi, onions, peas, beets, and carrots. Between the gardens and the chickens, they had a neat little ecosystem going. The chickens got the vegetable trimmings, and their manure was perfect fertilizer for the gardens.

Susie decided to go to New York to live. It was very hard for her, as well as for Lil, to overcome this separation. Less than a year later, Susie returned to live in Detroit.

Henry and Ilse felt they needed more space and asked to rent the entire house. They got it for five dollars more a month. The ownership of this house was a bit complicated. A young man, Mr. Letson, who as in the air force, was buying the house on a land contract from a woman, Mrs. Jordan. This all transpired during the war, and Mr. Letson's mother, who lived in Detroit, was looking after his business transactions.

Mr. Letson's grandmother, who lived south of Henry and Ilse on Garfield, collected the rent and was consulted when anything needed fixing.

Robert Gary Adler was born on February 6, 1943, in Munson Hospital in Traverse City, Michigan. The night before he was born, Henry and Ilse went to the movies. On the way home that night, they stopped in at the Moorsteins' for some coffee. Later, in the middle of the night, Henry had to take Ilse to the hospital. It had started to snow lightly, but by morning a full-blown blizzard was raging. Henry had to go to work right after the baby was born and had to leave the hospital before Ilse woke up—the doctor was late, and the nurses had given Ilse a heavy anesthetic. This baby gave Ilse many hours of bliss. While nursing him, he held on to her little finger, and the whole world around them disappeared.

Ilse's sister, Susie, who was then in Detroit, came to help. When they brought "Bobby" home, big brother and sister were entranced by him.

In 1944, when Bob was just over a year old, Mr. Letson, then a young air force man, was informed that he was to be shipped to the Far East. He hitched a ride to Detroit and then came to Traverse City. He told Henry and Ilse that since he did not know how much longer the war would last, he regretfully decided to sell the house. Since they lived there, he would give them first choice. However, while this was extremely decent of the man, it threw them into a tizzy.

Henry and Ilse were barely making it, living "hand to mouth," and they had absolutely no savings for a down payment. Henry went to the congregation for help. Not one of the wealthy home owners would loan them the money for a down payment. Mr. Rabinovitch, who had refused to help them with affidavits of support for their folks they had left behind, offered to buy the house and sell it to them. This would be on a land contract, for which no down payment was required.

Henry told Mr. Letson about the offer. Mr. Letson told Mrs. Jordan, from whom he had been buying the house. Happily, Mrs. Jordan then said, "If Henry Adler is good enough for Mr. Rabinovitch, he's good enough for me." She decided to sell them the house on a similar land contract. She asked them to pay five dollars more per month, to which they happily agreed.

While in the house on Garfield Avenue, Johnny (Steve) had many playmates and a large yard to play in. He started kindergarten at the old Oak Park School. He was very fond of Mrs. Mildred Pierce, who later also was Lil's and Bob's teacher. Steve always was a good student. At times, his school years were difficult for him because Ilse was ignorant of and oblivious to the phenomenon of peer pressure. Ilse forced him to wear the nice hand-me-down clothes they received from various members of their congregation instead of what he wanted to wear.

Bobby was about eighteen months old when he gave them all a big scare. Ilse was upstairs with him. He was at the head of the stairs and caught his foot in his pants. He tumbled down the stairs, head over heels. Ilse ran down the stairs, screaming, fearing he was badly hurt. He was all right, though. Steve and Lil were also there at the bottom of the stairs, and Ilse had to calm them all down. Ilse took Bob and the two other kids, all crying, and held them in her arms.

When Bob was two they discovered he was cross-eyed. An ophthalmologist operated on his eyes twice. He later said that Bob had almost no vision in his right eye, and the eye had turned because it was trying to compensate. Bob learned to live with this handicap, and he is able to drive, ski, and play ball in spite of it.

In 1946, when Bob was three, Ilse took the kids downtown. She left the boys in the barbershop and told Steve, then eight years old, to watch his kid brother while she took Lillian to the doctor just down the block.

When Ilse came back to the barbershop, no Bob! Ilse asked Steve where Bob was, and he said he did not know. Ilse was frantic. She had parked their car in the parking lot across the river. There was a rickety wooden bridge across the river, and the kids used to climb up on the railing. She imagined her baby already had fallen in the water.

Ilse retraced her steps to the doctor's office, but he was not there. Then she went into the dime store; she knew a lady who worked there. The lady said she had seen him, crying, and a gentleman had taken him by the hand and led him away. Ilse called the police, and they told her that he was already at home. Bob had told them his name, address, and telephone number. Bob also told them the telephone number of the factory where his daddy worked. They were amazed by how much this little three-year-old knew.

Many other events occurred during the nine years they lived at 223 Garfield Avenue. On Thanksgiving 1944, when Bob was only twenty months old, Lil came down with the measles. Steve also got them. Their doctor, who still made house calls in those days, came and gave Bob, the baby, a gamma globulin shot. He said this would protect him, so that even if he got the measles it would only be a mild case.

No sooner were the children recovered from the measles than they came down with whooping cough. This was followed by scarlatina, for which they had to be quarantined. Henry had to move out and stay with friends—he could only come to a window to visit.

By the time this siege was over, it was May. Ilse collapsed and became ill. Ilse had strep throat, a high fever, and all that goes with it. By the time she was able to get up, she was so weak that she could hardly walk out onto the screened porch to just sit there. Ilse was young, however, and got through it.

When they all had recovered from the bout with scarlatina, the county health nurse came to check on them. At that occasion, Ilse mentioned to her that Steve had begun to stammer. The nurse suggested that Ilse take him to see Dr. Mark Osterlin, the chief of pediatric services at the Munson Medical Center. He examined Steve and referred him to Miss Hazel Hardacre, a psychiatric social worker at the child guidance clinic.

Miss Hardacre used play therapy with Steve. She called Ilse in for a consultation. The first thing she told her was that Steve was as bright as a silver dollar. She then asked her to describe the living situation. Ilse told her that they led a hand-to-mouth existence with little left for extras. She said Henry just had managed to buy her the new dress she was wearing. When Ilse finished, Miss Hardacre said that she was definitely cut out to be a professional worker and encouraged Ilse in this vein. Ilse had just recently started to work for Dr. Wilcox. Miss Hardacre felt that this would reduce the tensions and stress to which Steve was responding.

Eventually, it was arranged for Lil to be seen at the child guidance clinic by a Miss Perskary. Both children have fond memories of those days. Even Bob wanted to get in on the fun. Much later in her career, Ilse learned the play-therapy philosophy and mode of action. In any event, it worked, and they were all better off for the therapy.

It was during that year that they were catapulted into home ownership. Their property consisted of twelve lots. A fellow worker approached Henry to buy one of the lots, since he wanted to build a house. Henry sold it to him, and the man started to build a basement. The neighbor lived in the basement for a year, while earning enough to begin completing the rest of the house.

Lil was a happy child, playing with all the neighborhood kids. In the summer they often packed a lunch and spent the day on the beach in Bryant Park. The first time, after she just had started to walk, she toddled into the water. She never was afraid and learned to swim very soon. She became an excellent swimmer, as are her brothers and her children. Everyone often reminisces about the summers at Bryant Park.

All three of Henry and Ilse's children learned swimming at Bryant Park through the Red Cross, Lil even learned lifesaving. Each year at the end of the season, the kids had to take a swimming exam. Ilse remembered the one Lil took at age ten. It was on Labor Day weekend. The water was pretty cold. She came out, shivering but proudly carrying the ribbon she had earned.

During these years, they met Ed Deake, who worked as a night watchman at the Tru-Fit Trousers factory. He was then already an elderly man. He was well read. Henry and he got along very well. Later on, he rented a cabin next door to them and became a surrogate grandfather to their children. They all liked him very much and missed him greatly when he died in 1950.

When Bob was four, Ilse took him to Detroit on a trip with a fellow worker. They went in the fellow worker's car. On the return trip, Ilse was driving and had a bad accident. They were taken to a hospital. Bob had been holding his arm. Ilse failed to ask at that time for an x-ray of his arm. The next day, in Traverse City, they found that he had a broken arm. This required surgery twice. Bob developed a keloid on his scar, which he nicknamed his "alligator".

The following summer Bob developed a lot of warts on his hands. The warts disappeared when he came down with scarlatina. He had such a high fever that he became delirious. In the delirium, he heard the sirens of a passing fire truck, and he screamed, "I didn't do it!"

When Bob started school, he loved it. He was a good student through all his school years. In fifth grade he had a favorite teacher, Miss Gladys Maxwell. He asked to invite her to his birthday party. Ilse did, and she came. She told us that this was the first time one of her pupils had invited her to a birthday party. She was very pleased and for years always asked about Bob whenever Ilse saw her.

Bobby learned easily but was never as good a student as was his potential. He was always curious and would challenge many a teacher if he did not agree with what had been taught in class.

In retrospect, Bob would have done better if the pattern of promotion beyond his grade level had been as common as it is now. Anyway, he did all the things his same-age schoolmates did. He was in scouting, played football, and skied.

Steve was a Boy Scout when he was ten and eleven. He went to the Boy Scout camp by a nearby lake at the supply road. They were invited to a "Indian powwow" one evening, and the scouts enacted a canoe landing with torches and a lot of singing. The following year, he went to a camp near Kalkaska.

When Bob became a Cub Scout, Ilse was the den mother, and Steve became the den chief—a family affair. Ilse helped Bobby more than she should have, but they were glad to complete the scouting.

Lil went into 4-H and had Mrs. Deo for an instructor. The 4-Hers went on several trips, one of which stands out. On the trip to Iowa, Lil scared the accompanying Mr. Olson and the host farmers to death by getting on a tractor and driving it into a field. For years afterward, whenever Ilse met Mr. Olson, he would speak to her about this feat. Lil went to the 4-H camp at Twin Lakes near Traverse City. She made many friends during these years.

In those days, Steve was still called "Johnny." He went to Detroit with Henry and met Stefan Schmidt, who had helped the family to escape from Nazi Europe. Steve was impressed, and when he was asked to be called by his middle name in the seventh grade (there were six Johns in the class), he willingly changed. Today he goes by J. Steve Adler.

Henry and Ilse had three fires during the nine years they lived at 223 Garfield. The first was set by five-year-old Steve, together with a friend, Danny Tanner. They were playing with matches in the backyard near the fence to the fairgrounds. The fire department had to come and put it out. Henry came home from work, and there was a general excitement. No one was injured, and the damage was minimal.

The next fire happened when Ilse's sister, who lived with them and slept on the screened-in back porch, woke up and saw the back shed lit up by flames. Susie had ironed the evening before and forgot to disconnect the iron. It had burned clear through the ironing board and fell on the floor. Susie woke up Henry and Ilse. Henry made Ilse take the two kids (this happened before Bob was born) out. Ilse went onto the back porch with them. Henry ran out and grabbed the hose. He had the fire out in no time. Susie told Ilse that she was standing there asleep, holding the kids by their hands. Of course, they had to buy a new ironing board.

The third fire happened when Henry and Ilse were in Detroit, and Susie was there with the children. She was talking on the telephone when a neighbor came to the door and asked if they had a hose. Susie said yes and continued with her telephone conversation. Then, finally, someone came and told her that the roof of their front porch was on fire. Luckily, the hose was all that was needed to put out the fire. It was later assumed that a bird must have picked up a smoldering cigarette butt and dropped it on the porch roof. Their fire insurance paid for the damage. Before they had it fixed, however, they sold the property to the city and started to move out with the help of friends and fellow workers.

In 1946, Ilse and Henry had three small children, and Ilse was trying to find some kind of work to contribute to household expenses. One afternoon Ilse was reading through the want ads in the *Record Eagle*. She jumped up and hollered, "This is finally a job for me!" There was an ad in the paper by a psychiatrist at the state hospital, who was looking for a person to translate medical material from German, French, Italian, Spanish, and Russian.

The next day Ilse tried to find the elusive Dr. Paul H. Wilcox, director of research. Ilse had to take her three-year-old baby with her because she didn't have a babysitter. They were sitting in Dr. Wilcox's office, waiting for him, and when he arrived, Ilse introduced herself and her son. Ilse told him that she came in response to his ad in the paper. She told him that she knew four of the five languages but was sorry that she couldn't help with Russian. Dr. Wilcox pulled out an article in German, handed it to her, and asked her to translate it. Ilse was able to do it, of course, but not very fast.

He was satisfied and asked her when she could start. Ilse explained to him that she had three small children, two in school, and that to take on a full-time job would be difficult. He was willing to take her on half time and allow her to work anytime that she could manage, as long as she worked twenty hours a week. They agreed that she was to start very soon (September 1946). He arranged for her to be hired as a state employee, but there was no opening under the appropriate title of library assistant. However, there was a position available as "housekeeper B"; this was offered, and she was to receive $129 per month.

Ilse started to work and soon discovered that her medical background of two years at the University of Vienna was by far not enough. She realized that she needed to study the subject matter before she could complete translations that made sense. Thus, Ilse embarked on a tutored study of psychiatry, neurology, and biochemistry, which all were necessary to help her understand what she was reading.

Before long, Dr. Wilcox wanted her to work full time. Ilse hired housekeepers and became more involved in her job.

Henry worked for Tru-Fit Trousers until the end of 1946. He had become the floor boss. At that time, Ilse had already gotten a job at the state hospital.

It was announced that Tru-Fit Trousers was going to close for a year. Mr. Neiman offered to keep Henry on the payroll. His job was to look after the empty factory. They were planning to come back in the spring and reopen the shop.

Henry, feeling very insecure about this situation, began nurse's training. Henry was hired by the state hospital in January 1947. As it later turned out, becoming state employees was one of their many lucky breaks and choices they made along the way.

Henry and Ilse had different assignments and worked different hospital shifts. This helped them to maintain their family without too much outside help. Yet they had a number of helpers. One of them was "Grandma" Mitchell, who was good in her way with the kids but had no skill in nutrition. She fed the kids a lot of starchy foods. Later, when they found out that she had charged food to their grocer and sent it home to her family, they fired her.

As mentioned before, Henry started at the Traverse City State Hospital in 1947 as an attendant nurse. He was immediately sent to work on hall 6, which was the most mentally disturbed male ward. Within three years, he had advanced to the highest rank as an attendant nurse and was very happy to work with his patients and his fellow workers. He refused to write a civil service exam for supervisor because he didn't want to push a pencil behind a desk; rather, he preferred work with patients.

Due to his painful experiences as a concentration camp inmate, Henry was eminently equipped for the difficult job of dealing with disturbed, unhappy creatures. Throughout the years of his work, he acquired a reputation as a thoughtful, kind, and gentle person. This fit with his basic personality, which was more important than any academic training. Over twenty years after his retirement, some of his former patients stopped him on the street and wanted to talk to him.

In December 1948, they heard from Ellie (Safier) in Detroit that she had skiing equipment for the children. One Sunday at noon, while together in bed, reading the funny papers, they decided on the spur of the moment to drive to Detroit to pick up the skiing gear. They got up and got dressed in a hurry. Ilse boiled some eggs, made a few sandwiches, and off they went. It was a nice sunny day. It was, however, cold, and every twig and every blade of grass was encased in ice that glittered like a thousand diamonds. It was before the days of expressways, and it took a long time to get as far as Pontiac, Michigan. There, they stopped at a restaurant to get warm and eat something.

When they got into Detroit, they had to split up. Henry took Lil and Ilse to stay with Susie, who lived on the other side of town from Ellie. Henry and the boys slept at Ellie's. In the morning, bright and early, Henry had to come and pick up Lil and Ilse to have breakfast at Ellie's. Ellie fixed sunny-side-up eggs in a special pan from Europe. This impressed the children to no end. After breakfast, they loaded up the skiing equipment and started the drive home. They had not gotten farther than Highland Park, Michigan, when it started to snow. It was a light snowfall at first, but the farther north they went, the heavier it snowed, until they were in a regular blizzard. Henry and Ilse took turns driving in near zero visibility. When they got to Cadillac, they stopped and called the hospital since they knew they would not make it home in time to go to work. Henry's supervisor told him not to come to work and to rest up as soon as they got home. Steve recalled that reaching a fairly steep hill, during the last few miles near Traverse City, they had get out of the car to push it up the slippery slope. They also used sand from a roadside barrel to improve traction. Henry was so glad to have made it home without an accident on the icy roads, He went to work, anyway, after a brief rest, for half a shift.

This crazy trip was a subject of conversation for years to come. They had gotten the ski equipment so that the kids could learn to ski. They took lessons from Peppy Teichner, a famous Austrian skier who also came to live in Traverse City. This took place at a low hill on US 31 South, where there now stand a few fast-food places.

In 1949, the city planned to build a new Oak Park School. The city attorney approached them and asked if they were willing to sell part of their property for the new school. They said yes, and he asked for a purchase option. Soon, he returned and asked for an option on the entire property. They again agreed and were excited about the prospect of selling the house and land.

Soon after the agreement, the city attorney came and wanted to know how much they wanted for whole property. They consulted several people regarding the value of the property. After talking it over with each other, they decided, since this was going to be a new school for all three of their children, they did not want to hold up the city. They asked for ten thousand dollars, which was less than what they learned was the land value. They had time to vacate the premises and find a new house, the house on 822 Washington Street.

They bought the house at 822 Washington Street and paid all their outstanding bills. They still had enough left over so that Henry could get a new suit (his first one since arriving in the USA). Their friends and fellow workers helped them move, and they started to work on the house. It needed a lot of refurbishing. They were all moved in by the beginning of 1950.

THE HOUSE AT 822 WASHINGTON STREET

When they moved into the house at 822 Washington, it was arranged as a two-apartment building. There was a second kitchen on the second floor, above the current kitchen. This was removed. They took out the water pipes and the sink. They made this upstairs kitchen into a third bedroom. There was a full bathroom upstairs, with a hardwood parquet floor. It was in a space that once may have been an upstairs bedroom. They had the bathroom floor covered with Congoleum. They installed shelves in a closet off the upstairs bathroom to make it into a linen closet. Downstairs, there was only a toilet and a wash basin in a powder room off the parlor. They made this parlor into the master bedroom. With the help of fellow workers, they moved the bathroom wall and installed a shower cabinet. As one entered the kitchen from the dining room, there was a cabinet on the wall to the right, and there was a sink and a stove with space in between. There was a window above the sink. On the south wall was a window and a refrigerator. Next to the refrigerator was a small window with a chest-high dividing wall to the back room. The back room had a door to the outside and a staircase that led to the upstairs. There also was a door from the kitchen into the back room. Next to the dining room door was a door to the basement.

They rented a sander, but when they tried to smooth down the floor, they found it full of knot holes. They painted the floor. Eventually, they acquired a sisal rug, and that covered many a problem. In 1950, they had hardwood floors installed in down-stairs rooms with Congoleum in the kitchen and bathroom.

Much has changed over the years. When one entered the house from the street side there was a porch and a mud room and then straight into the small anteroom and into the dining room. To the left there was a door into the living room.

When Steve was thirteen, in 1951, a group of Jewish men from Detroit decided to arrange for him to have a bar mitzvah. These men came regularly to vacation at the home of Dr. Leonard Sidlow on the peninsula north of Traverse City. There, they had their *kibbutz*, where they studied and enhanced their Jewish identity.

A young rabbi among these men prepared Steve for his bar mitzvah ceremony. They also arranged for Rabbi Morris Adler of their Detroit congregation to officiate in Traverse City. Among these men was Judge Rubiner. He was invited to the altar and gave a short speech. The judge said that forty years ago on that very date, he had had his own bar mitzvah in this same synagogue in Traverse City. Steve's bar mitzvah event was written up in the *Jewish News* in Detroit, with a few significant mistakes. Ilse wrote a letter to their editor, suggesting corrections, but there was no response.

Steve continued to be a good student. In high school he also had a newspaper delivery route with about 150 customers. Later, when he was old enough, he worked at Kroger's food store as a shelf stocker and carry-out boy. Before his high school graduation, he took his then-girlfriend, Helen Auldrich, to his high school prom. There is a picture of them in prom clothes. Steve graduated from high school in 1956.

Steve went to Northwestern Michigan College (NMC), the local community college. While in college, he took a job as pin setter at a nearby bowling alley. One evening he forgot his lunch, and Ilse took it to him. Ilse was astonished that he could study with all that racket going on around him, but it did not seem to bother him.

When Steve graduated from NMC, he received a small scholarship and went on to the University of Michigan. There, he found it rough going since all the other students there were the cream of the crop. He lived in a co-op house, where he met an international group of fellow students. Once when Ilse visited him there, she met a Sikh with beard and turban, wearing a white apron as he took his turn at KP. Ilse also met some Chinese, French, Indian, Pakistani, and German students, who also lived in the co-op.

Lil was a good student and liked school. After graduation from high school in 1958, she got herself a job, which she liked very much, in Glen Arbor. In the fall, she went to Wayne State University in Detroit. There, she lived with her aunt Susie, who had moved to Detroit from New York. Lil's experience there was disappointing. She soon came back to Traverse City and went to NMC, the local community college.

The following summer she worked again in Glen Arbor, and she met Daniel Ostendorf. Later, she went to Cincinnati to meet his family, and they became engaged. She was still working in Glen Arbor when the air force transferred Dan to Newfoundland.

While Dan was in Newfoundland, his father died suddenly. Henry and Ilse went with Lil to pick up Dan, who had flown to Kinchloe Air Force Base. The next day, Lil and Dan went to Cincinnati for the funeral.

After graduation from high school in 1961, Bob went on to college at Michigan State University. He graduated from MSU with a degree in political science. Finding that he was 4F (ineligible for the army draft), he went off to Aspen, Colorado, ski bumming and working as a carpenter during the summer.

Bob held a variety of jobs in Aspen. He met Betty, now his wife, in Aspen. He brought Betty and her sister to Traverse City to meet the Adler family.

In 1965, they had to rebuild the front porch and porch roof because of an invasion of carpenter ants.

In 1966, they remodeled the kitchen cabinets and appliances. Also in the 1960s, they built a screened-in back porch onto the kitchen, which they enjoyed very much. This included changing the door to the outside, the window in the kitchen, and changing the arrangement in the utility room (back room), which now has the washer and dryer.

In 1975, they paneled the dining room, and a year before that they had the living room paneled and more shelves installed.

In 1975, Henry and Ilse started traveling to Phoenix, Arizona, to spend the winters. They moved to Scottsdale in 1986. Fred Schneider investigated available apartments for them. He recommended the Indian Bend apartment complex. Steve inspected and approved it. Steve also rented furniture for them so that when they arrived, all they needed to do was to unpack the boxes with bedding, make the beds, and go to sleep. The next morning Nancy Schneider came to see them. They went shopping together and had breakfast. Henry and Ilse had a two-bedroom apartment with two baths, two walk-in closets, a living room (with space for a dining room set), and a fully equipped kitchen. Off the living room there was a patio from which it was only a few steps to the swimming pool and hot tub. The landscaping was beautiful and kept up nicely. They liked it there very much and had quite a few friends in the apartment complex. Weather permitting, they lived in swimwear and robes most of the time. Shopping was easily accessible, and since neither of them drove anymore, they used taxicabs for transportation. They had good household help, and life was easy and pleasant there. They leased the apartment year-round so they had no furniture to move. They left many things there when traveling back and forth from Michigan. The management provided many extras, such as aqua aerobics three times a week, a coffee klatch three times a week, free movies twice weekly, and a brunch once a month. The rent for their apartment included utilities, maintenance, and a covered parking space. They had a guest room, and in it Ilse had a computer desk.

In 1976 in Traverse City, while Henry and Ilse were in Arizona, Steve and Daniel paneled the two upstairs front bedrooms and added some new electrical wiring. They came during spring break for Easter and Passover and did this as a surprise home improvement for Henry and Ilse. Lil had to take care of all the kids since Carole was home recovering from surgery. In addition, Lil made a Seder with Darin's (Steve's oldest son) help and advice.

Henry and Ilse were very happy with their children and grandchildren. They developed a tradition of having an annual family reunion at Thanksgiving. The family took turns hosting, when after a few years, it got a little too much for the oldsters. It became a tradition to travel to wherever the host lived. At several of these occasions, Henry and Ilse had family portraits taken. In 1993, Henry and Ilse hosted Thanksgiving in Traverse City, at Bob's suggestion. Bob and Betty were to host that year. It had become a major family event. It included the Thanksgiving family reunion and the wedding of Lil's son Mark and Tracie. Lil also assisted, as Mark and Tracie's wedding was on the Friday after Thanksgiving at the Bower's Harbor Inn.

The house in Traverse City is now their children's; they conveyed the home and management of their finances to the children many years ago. Henry and Ilse had a "life lease" and were able to make several trips together in addition to alternating months in Traverse City and Scottsdale.

ILSE ADLER—WORK HISTORY, PLUS

The interruption of Ilse's education lasted until she was safely in the United States and had begun the job at the Traverse City State Hospital. She was able to get this job because of her language and medical background.

One of the social workers told her about college extension classes being offered locally. Ilse was naive and totally unaware of the implications involved in the different college extension courses and their registration prerequisites. She was only impressed by the fact that one was a class in psychology.

Ilse enrolled in a school, which demanded that she relinquish her credentials and was not willing to return her original papers. Many years later, they gave her photocopies of them. What she did find out many years later was that they had sent her certificate of graduation from the Realgymnasium to a place in Washington, DC, to be translated.

The translation did not include the last three years of her schooling. This gave her credit only for middle school. The translator had not read the top line of her certificate of graduation, which read REALGYMNASIUM DES VEREINES DEUTSCHE MAESCHEN MITTELSCHULE. She found this out too late to claim compensation for the omission. She felt it cost her literally millions of dollars in earning capacity.

Ilse intrepidly continued her endeavor to complete her interrupted education. She enrolled at Northwestern Michigan College (NMC), the local community college. Ilse earned an associate's degree, which she felt she should have already had on the basis of finishing the Realgymnasium curriculum.

Meanwhile, while working at her job in psychiatry, she had studied on her own. Ilse studied the subject matter needed to make sense of her document translations and abstracts.

The subjects included neurology, neurophysiology, biochemistry, and, of course, psychiatry. These subjects were studied under the guidance of her then-boss and mentor Paul Wilcox, MD.

When Dr. Wilcox hired her, he was the director of research at the state hospital. He was also the secretary-treasurer of the Electroshock Research Association (ESRA). Dr. Wilcox annually wrote a chapter on electroshock therapies for the publication *Progress on Neurology and Psychiatry*. Ilse's job consisted of translating and abstracting foreign language articles pertaining to this work.

When Ilse started the job, she became a Michigan state employee. In 1950, the state laid her off. This was the result of a retrenchment program under which all "nonessential" jobs were eliminated. Ilse's job as a library assistant was deemed nonessential. However, the Electroshock Research Association hired her to continue with their work until their funds ran out. Ilse lost this job too, when the ESRA (Dr. Paul Wilcox) finally could no longer afford her services.

So there Ilse was without a job. She tried every which way to find work but was overspecialized or overqualified for those available. So the family decided to go on a trip to New York. This was one of their special trips taken "on a shoestring" (in retrospect, according to Ilse, a "very frayed shoestring").

71

In May 1953, Ilse decided, as a last resort, to apply for a job at the state hospital as an attendant nurse. This was over the objections of the then-director of nursing, Miss Orcutt. With the help of Dr. Sheets, the superintendent, Ilse was hired.

Ilse was assigned to cottage 35, the state hospital geriatric ward for women. Most of these patients were quite out of contact and/or seriously disturbed. It was a hard job for her to get used to. Her fellow workers were covertly hostile because, she thought, of Miss Orcutt's notion that she was overqualified and not well suited to an attendant nurse's job. Ilse asked too many questions about patient care. According to Ilse, she was dealt with open contempt and disregard for her welfare.

In her first evaluation, she got a questionable grade. Her supervisor wrote that she wasn't good enough at washing the walls and windows. Additionally, she spent too much time talking to the patients. Henry was upset about this evaluation. Henry promptly went to see Dr. Sheets to intervene in what he thought was Miss Orcutt's strategy to get her fired. In July, Henry and Ilse traveled to Chicago to meet her cousins George and Edith Roth from New Zealand. Miss Orcutt insisted that Ilse work a half day on the Fourth of July, after which they drove to Chicago.

When in-service training classes were announced, Ilse signed up. Ilse knew that she could start on rotations away from cottage 35. Ilse tried to apply on the ward what she learned in classes. This was met with rejection and derision. Soon, Ilse was put into an in-service training class for attendants, and she rotated to a number of different wards. Later, as a social worker, these nursing experiences came in handy. Ilse had an inside view of the politics and foibles of ward attendants. Ilse never regretted having this learning experience.

In 1955, the superintendent, Dr. Phillip Sheets, suffered a stroke and died. The assistant superintendent, Dr. Nickles, was promoted to acting superintendent, and one of the young doctors, whom Ilse had met when he was a psychiatric resident, was promoted to assistant superintendent. He had known Ilse when she worked with Dr. Wilcox. The assistant superintendent felt that her talents were wasted, working as an attendant nurse. He set her up in an office to work on a variety of tasks. At that time, the "medieval" insurance companies had begun to accept claims for mental illness hospitalization. The stenography pool became flooded with insurance claim forms to fill out. Ilse was asked to assist with these insurance claim forms. In addition, Ilse was given the job of writing case abstracts of patients transferred to other institutions. This gave Ilse an opportunity to familiarize herself with the order in which items relevant to a case were filed.

One of the doctors who knew her and trusted her judgment gave her the task of ghostwriting diagnoses. He reviewed them and, if satisfied, signed them. This was extremely valuable training and preparation for Ilse's eventual promotion to social worker.

Clifford Lindstrom, the director of social services, "borrowed" Ilse to write ten or twelve social histories. They had been left undone by a social worker who had returned to school to finish her master's degree. This started Ilse's career toward becoming a full-fledged social worker.

This too gave Ilse insight into what sources were needed to compile a social history. Ilse learned to distinguish between good and poor initial interviews by the various doctors. It helped her understand the inner workings of the whole system. Ilse was asked to help with an examination of the classifications of the psychiatric literature in the hospital medical library. The users of this library found that the Dewey Decimal System was inadequate for classifying the growing complexity in the literature. Ilse went to the medical library at the general hospital and got reprints of their medical library articles. She noticed that the general hospital librarians used color coding on their records. Ilse introduced this method of coping with the expanding variety of topics in the psychiatric literature. She transplanted her knowledge gained while working with Dr. Paul Wilcox to this psychiatric literature classification endeavor.

Ilse was also taking classes at NMC to further her education. Eventually, she took civil service exams in the area of social work. In 1959, Ilse graduated from NMC with an associate's degree. She pursued further education to earn a BA degree. Ilse was working as a social worker, and her assignment was the geriatric mental health service. In 1961, Professor Christopher Sower of Michigan State University (MSU) offered to teach a course in community organization at the hospital. It could be taken for credit on a graduate level, undergraduate level, or for auditing. Ilse was interested and signed up. After the first session, Ilse asked Professor Sower if a paper was required when the course was taken for credit. Professor Sower asked on what level Ilse was taking the course. Ilse told him that she was working toward a BA. Ilse then showed him a spreadsheet that she had made for her work as a social worker. On this spreadsheet Ilse had listed the first hundred patients consecutively admitted to her service. She had made rubrics for relevant information about their background and had made up a code to use on punched cards (the forerunners of computer filings). Professor Sower asked who had designed this study. Ilse told him that she had done it on her own. She explained that she had learned this method while working for Dr. Paul Wilcox. Professor Sower said he felt that Ilse did not need a BA and that she was working at a graduate level. Professor Sower suggested that Ilse go to Michigan State University and apply for admission to the graduate school of sociology. Professor Sower said Ilse should tell them her story and that this was his recommendation. Ilse was admitted to the MSU graduate school of sociology. While all this transpired, Ilse worked full time, ran the Adler household, and took care of her family. It was a full life. In order to work toward her master's degree, Ilse enrolled in a seminar that was held Wednesday evenings on the MSU campus in East Lansing. Henry and Ilse commuted between Traverse City and Lansing for the entire school term. Henry went to a movie while Ilse was in class.

Ilse was introduced to Professor Honigsheim. He had her do a research paper at home. Professor Honigsheim gave her all sorts of books for the background study. Ilse did very well and completed the paper. Ilse then started on her thesis. The thesis was designed to explore the background and social matrix of one hundred consecutively admitted teenagers at the Traverse City State Hospital. It was to find indicators for the development of their behavioral pathology or mental and/or emotional difficulties that led to their hospitalization.

Difficulties with Ilse's advisor eventually scuttled her thesis. The advisor from the state hospital staff was a stickler for academic detail. He left Ilse totally discouraged after spending hours and hours on work that he then found inadequate. As a result, Ilse did not finish her work toward a master's degree.

Despite not finishing her thesis, the Civil Service Administration accepted Ilse's educational status as the equivalent of a bachelor's degree and permitted her to write the examination for social worker. Ilse also traveled to Lansing for an oral examination. A funny thing occurred at that time. After being questioned by two young assistants, Maggie Culver, the director of the State Department of Social Service, came in and wanted to know what Ilse thought of the written exam. Ilse had met Maggie years earlier when Maggie was a member of the social service staff at the Traverse City State Hospital. Ilse told her that she thought the test had not specifically tested for social work skills but that it rated her overall educational status and her personality using a partial MMPI. Maggie wanted to know what "MMPI" stood for. Ilse told her, wide-eyed, that MMPI meant Minnesota Multiple Personality Inventory. Maggie then asked where Ilse had learned about the MMPI. Ilse told her that

Dr. Kay Wilcox had tested her using it and had explained what it meant. When Ilse returned and told her boss, Cliff Lindstrom, about this conversation, he laughed out loud and said, "Do you know what you did?" When Ilse said no, Cliff Lindstrom informed her that Maggie had designed the test Ilse had taken and was proud of it.

Ilse became a full-fledged social worker. In the years until her retirement, Ilse did a lot of the work she had aimed at when she started to study medicine. Her goal had been to become a psychiatrist. Ilse did individual and group therapy and eventually founded the Traverse City Friendship Center (a mental health halfway house).

Ilse gained a lot of knowledge, especially from the extension courses in cultural anthropology and community organization she took at NMC.

Annual trips to meetings of the American Psychiatric Association also enhanced Ilse's abilities. So did Ilse's participation in the Journal Club at the Traverse City State Hospital. Ilse felt that her most profitable education came from Dr. Robert E. Pearson, who supervised her individual and group therapy work. Ilse worked to keep up with the progress of scientific advances at each stage of her career.

Beginning with her work with Dr. Wilcox, Ilse subscribed to the *Digest of Neurology and Psychiatry*, published by the Institute of Living in Hartford, Connecticut. Later, Ilse subscribed to a Canadian publication of psychiatric materials. Ilse did not renew the various subscriptions after her retirement in 1976. She presented many of the papers from these publications to the staff at the Journal Club. Ilse also presented some of her own work, such as the papers she produced for her college classes, as well as translations of German or Italian material she had found during her many trips to the medical library in Ann Arbor, Michigan.

In the late 1940s or the early '50s, Professor Ugo Cerletti sent Dr. Wilcox a copy of his book, published in Italy. This was about Professor Ugo Cerletti's work at the Neurology and Psychiatric Clinic in Rome. In it, Professor Ugo Cerletti described how he had come to use electric current to induce convulsions and how this method was applied for the first time in a human patient. Ilse translated this chapter in the history of ECT psychiatry. The book was donated as a part of the Wilcox library to Northwestern University by Katherine Wilcox, professor emeritus.

Dr. Kay Wilcox, wife of Dr. Paul Wilcox, was a psychologist. Some of their four boys and Ilse would make trips during the year to the medical library in Ann Arbor. There, many of the foreign language medical journals were available. They would diligently peruse them. Ilse's job was to translate, abstract, and condense the material they found. They each wrote their findings on punch cards, using a code Dr. Wilcox had developed so they could be sorted. The punched cards contained the abstracts of the various papers. Ilse later realized that this method was a forerunner of computer searches.

Ilse's work at the state hospital was interesting and exciting. Dr. Wilcox, the psychiatrist for whom Ilse worked, had become world famous. He was in charge of the training of psychiatric residents and also had visitors from all over the world. Two of these visitors were psychiatrists from Nuremberg, Germany. These visitors, also well known in their own right, came to study with Dr. Wilcox and observe his treatment methods.

One afternoon, it was raining hard. Ilse was driving along Front street helping Steve deliver his newspapers. They saw two rain-soaked men walking toward Shadowland, a bar and restaurant. They were the two doctors from Germany. Ilse was also the interpreter for Dr. Wilcox and these psychiatrists from Germany since their English was poor. Ilse offered them a lift, which was gratefully accepted. The doctors couldn't get over the fact that she was driving such a "luxurious" car (a 1949 Ford, four-door sedan.) They remarked that in Germany, only high-ranking business persons or officials would drive cars like this. Ilse explained that in the United States, many ordinary working people had similar cars.

In the same year, the American Field Service sponsored a group of German visitors. Some students and the mayor of Ulm came to Traverse City. Ilse was hired to accompany the group as an interpreter. They went to all sorts of interesting places. At the Leland School for Boys, they were invited for lunch. The milk was served in pint bottles with a cardboard closure that had to be pushed down to open the bottle. The mayor of Ulm, not familiar with this bottle cap, pushed down too hard, and the milk sprayed all over him. He, being a very proper German, was so embarrassed that he couldn't stop talking about how clumsy he was. It was difficult for the others to keep from laughing. For years afterward, the mayor of Ulm sent Ilse New Year's cards from "Ulm on the Danube."

Ilse was also called on to interpret for the mayor of Ulm when he met with Senator William Milliken in Traverse City. There were several interesting questions the mayor asked the senator. It was only a few years after the end of the war, and some of the questions touched on subjects that were difficult to broach. Ilse was impressed by their conversation.

A few years after their visit, one of the German psychiatrists sent Ilse a paper that he had written, titled "Die Phenomenologie der Vergreisung," or "The Phenomenology of Aging." Ilse proceeded to translate it and presented it in Journal Club. Ilse sent it to the *American Journal of Psychiatry* for publication. They said that they needed permission from the author to print the translation. Unfortunately, Dr. Wagner had died, and when Ilse wrote to his widow for permission, she never responded. As a result, this paper was only to presented in Journal Club.

Dr. Wilcox, his wife Dr, Kay Wilcox and Ilse took several trips to Ann Arbor. All three read and abstracted articles from the many foreign journals available in the medical library. Dr. Wilcox and his wife would read the English, and Ilse would read the German, French, Italian, and so on. One of these was the first report of a Swiss company that found the strange effects of diethyl amide lysergic acid, or LSD, as it later became known. It described the strange effect it had on persons when they were exposed to only micrograms of the drug. They described vivid hallucinations. Ilse felt it was important to translate this article into the English language. When Ilse translated this paper by Hoffman, she felt that these hallucinations described resembled phenomena observed in some of their patients and that it might eventually yield procedures to study therapeutic measures. This was actually done and reported at a round-table discussion at one of the APA meetings in 1955. As Ilse had anticipated, in later years the drug was used by psychiatrists to produce an artificial psychosis. They then proceeded to attempt to treat this artificial psychosis with various tranquilizers that had become known. At first, tranquilizers were used in Europe in the early fifties and then, later, in this country. Tranquilizers, such as Serpasil and Thorazine, were coming into use at the Traverse City State Hospital. They produced dramatic effects. Some of the very seriously disturbed schizophrenic patients miraculously became capable of normalized behavior and speech. This in itself produced problems, as there were only a few professional staff available to listen and respond to them.

One of the hospital physicians, Dr. T. J. Ferguson, who had promoted the use of tranquilizers, was interviewed by the author Paul de Kruif. Paul de Kruif had written a book about Dr. Ferguson titled *A Man against Insanity*. The book became quite popular and later was condensed by *Reader's Digest* and appeared in issues of the *Reader's Digest*, published in many languages. This resulted in a flood of mail from all over the world, begging Dr. Ferguson to take on their respective patients. Ilse was asked to translate and answer the letters that were in her fluent languages.

Dr. Wilcox was also approached by Paul de Kruif. However, Dr. Wilcox refused him because of the flamboyant way the story of Dr. Ferguson was written.

Working with Dr. Wilcox provided Ilse a one-on-one thorough training and psychiatric education. The work Ilse did for Dr. Wilcox gave her the opportunity to read many articles in psychiatry in addition to the ones she was doing for him. Ilse learned a great deal about the history of psychiatry and even more about Dr. Wilcox's own applied principles of therapy. For example, as Dr. Wilcox's assistant with the Electroshock Research Association, Ilse prepared a number of bulletins that were mimeographed and sent to the members of the association. In order to assemble these bulletins they would lay out stacks of the pages on a large library table in the medical library and staff room. Dr. Wilcox would corral several of his patients. They were in sufficient control, so that under Ilse's supervision they could assemble the bulletins, staple them together, and put them in envelopes ready for mailing. This was a quasi-occupational therapy undertaking. This was similar to the service of a number of patients who were typing with Ilse in the office.

When Dr. Wilcox retired from state employment, he continued to employ Ilse in the same capacity. At one time, Ilse had to set up the Adler living room as an office to do all the work.

HENRY ADLER—WORK HISTORY, PLUS

When they arrived in the USA in 1939, at the end of the Great Depression, jobs were scarce. In addition, lacking language and saleable skills, jobs were not available for them. When they came to Traverse City, the situation improved. Henry's first steady job was in the garment industry, as described earlier. Eventually, Henry and Ilse both became state employees in Michigan. Henry worked as a state employee until his retirement in 1973.

Henry studied and became an attendant nurse at the Traverse City State Hospital. Right after he was hired, he was assigned work on hall 6. This was the ward for the most mentally disturbed men.

In those days, only sedatives and segregation were used as treatment methods. The attendant crew with whom he worked was mostly farmers from the surrounding area. They often had barely a high school education. They were simple and unsophisticated but strong, burly men. The attendants had not been taught even the rudiments about their charges' problems. Attendants did not understand that mental illness often meant a loss of personhood. Attendants were not told that patients should to be treated in such a way that their pride and dignity were not injured.

Segregation was used for double incontinent patients, who often could not keep their clothes on. They were kept in a place called a "specialing room." There, an attendant sat at the door to keep the patients from wandering into the ward. This was to make it easier to clean them up and clean up the excrement. This attendant had a pail and mop next to him.

Another method was necessary for highly disturbed, combative persons. They were put in a so-called "strong room" with only a mattress on the floor. They would get a tray with their food. The rest of the patients were taken to a dining room adjacent to the ward. There, they sat at tables with only a tin plate and a spoon to eat. After much work, Henry arranged for the patients to be given a full set of cutlery at their meals. This cutlery had to be counted after every meal, before the patients were returned to the ward. The ward also had an open-air porch, where, in good weather, patients could move around freely and smoke. Verbal communication was difficult and often totally impossible with these poor wretches. Often, strong-arm techniques were necessary, although highly distasteful for Henry, whose sensitive nature had been finely honed by his days in the concentration camp. This experience, although painful, made him eminently well suited to his job. Within three years, he had worked his way up to ward supervisor and was given an assignment on hall 12. Here, he had semidisturbed and younger patients, with whom communication became easier and more prevalent.

Henry was a maverick, always introducing new ideas and methods. For ten years in a row, Henry and Ilse traveled with the Wilcoxes to the annual meeting of the American Psychiatric Association. This had become financially feasible through Henry's employment by Reuben Reiter, the exhibitor of Dr. Wilcox's latest models of electrostimulation equipment at the scientific exhibit accompanying the meetings. On these occasions, Henry spoke with many of the psychiatrists and learned a great deal.

On these trips, Dr. Wilcox stopped at various clinics to demonstrate his methods. Ilse, on the other hand, attended lectures at the meetings and always returned home full of new ideas, which she shared with the professional staff at the hospital, giving reports at the Journal Club. This, however, was not always accepted with the same enthusiasm that Henry and Ilse brought home with them.

The hospital had a residency training program for physicians who wanted to become psychiatrists. Among these residents were many foreign doctors with great language difficulties. Since language is the principal medium for psychiatric treatment, Henry found himself in the role of interpreter. Most of the patients came from rural areas and often had less than a high school education. In addition to their psychiatric problems, many used slang expressions that left the foreign doctors at a loss. The patients, on the other hand, could not understand the broken English of the residents. Henry and Ilse urged the hospital to require the foreign residents to enroll in ESL classes (English as a Second Language). This, however, was not always successful.

Henry's last assignment was as chief on cottage 28, an open prerelease ward, where patients were prepared to return to their home community. Here too Henry started an innovation by allowing the patients to get their own medication from the medicine cabinet. This raised a lot of eyebrows and created much controversy. Henry's argument was that when these men were on their own, there would be no one to give their medications to them.

In those days, hospital staff was involved in the statewide and nationwide efforts to reduce the "warehousing" of persons who no longer needed or no longer could profit from active psychiatric treatment. At the same time the hospitals failed to teach the general public about the pitfalls that were inevitable when patients were released without preparation for living on their own in adult foster homes, rented apartments, or elsewhere. They had the security of the hospital environment, its supervision, and the various social activities the hospital provided. These things the released patients had to seek for themselves. Thus, Henry and Ilse saw a number of former patients who could not adjust to their new situations and roamed the streets. This caused much hostility on the part of the general public, combined with the "second-class citizenship" customarily attributed to mental patients.

When Henry retired he was given a sort of tongue-in-cheek recognition as an innovator by being presented a certificate of Chief of Rule Breaking and Disobedience. However, he was considered so unique that no one was able to fill his shoes.

ILSE AND THE CREATION OF THE FRIENDSHIP CENTER

Here is how and why the Friendship Center was created. As a social worker, Ilse had been involved in preparing patients for return to their home communities. In the case of quite a few of these candidates for release, they had been in the hospital so long that either there was no family left to accept them, or the family simply refused to have this chronic patient return.

Thus, many were placed in adult foster care or left to their own devices. The apartment rentals available to these marginally adjusted persons were few and rather shoddy. The landlords/landladies were only interested in the income and did not care about or were ill equipped to deal with these ex-patients' social needs.

There were many failures. The former patients returned to the hospital with the recurring complaints that there was nothing to do and no place to go outside the hospital. This gave Ilse the idea that a place was needed where there was something to do, where the former patients would not be regimented and told what to do and when. Ilse discussed this idea with the physicians, with her fellow workers, and with the hospital superintendent, Dr. Philip B. Smith. The superintendent was completely supportive. He told her to go ahead and recruit the support of the community.

In this endeavor, Ilse had help from a rather unexpected source—the director of the Traverse City Senior Center. The director had essentially thrown out some of former mental patients who had come to the Senior Center. They were not creating any trouble, but she simply did not want any impaired persons in *her* Senior Center. Additionally, she did not allow anyone in a wheelchair or with a cast on a broken limb. It appeared that her philosophy was to "protect" her seniors from any reminder of their frailty or their mortality. As a result, she was perfectly willing to assist Ilse in rallying members of the community to serve on a steering committee to develop a separate drop-in center for the former mental patients. Ilse accepted her assistance and ignored her reasons.

Then Ilse embarked on this most amazing task. Every one of the people Ilse approached for cooperation exclaimed, "Yes! This is what we need in Traverse City!" They promised to serve on the steering committee. There were ministers, the chief of police, the fire chief, several attorneys, and interested citizens.

They all agreed that a suitable location was needed. A real estate agent sent Ilse to Bill Votruba. Bill pledged the rent-free use of his dance studio in downtown Traverse City. He also provided free heat and water. He left a piano there for their use. The dance studio consisted of a huge ballroom with large mirrors on the walls and two adjoining smaller rooms. There also were two rooms across the hall, suitable for office space.

A member of the steering committee got secondhand carpeting from a local restaurant that had just put in new carpeting. Volunteers installed the carpeting. Several items of furniture were donated, including some from the hospital. These also were moved in by volunteers. A local grocer, Jerry Olson, donated a case of coffee, sugar, and milk. Friendship Center was ready for business. The Friendship Center opened on September 17, 1973. Wilda Schlessman, director of in-service training of nursing personnel, a true friend, was an invaluable helper with the preparations for this event . Wilda, also the director of occupational therapy, and Ilse were permitted to work at the center as detached state hospital employees. The superintendent, Dr. Philip B. Smith, assisted them in every possible way. Dr. Smith encouraged them to apply for a grant from the Michigan Department of Mental Health. They received a grant that allowed them to start with a budget of $4,800. They had funding to hire a secretary and purchase office supplies.

The opening was covered by a local TV station. As a result, Ilse was invited to speak to several groups and was interviewed by another TV station. These community contacts encouraged further donations of money. Other donated items poured in. They received an electric stove, a refrigerator, coffeemakers, serving utensils, and many more items. The nicest surprise came when their own clients began to contribute things and also volunteered to take care of certain chores, such as sweeping and keeping the sidewalk clear of snow.

Volunteers were the backbone of the operation. They were recruited from the community and trained by Friendship Center staff. Ilse's philosophy was to provide a low-key, low-pressure atmosphere, where staff as well as volunteers would listen and respond to the healthy expressions of the clients. This was without probing or questioning and did not attempt to do therapy. This let the environment be therapeutic.

They hoped that the volunteers would be role models of socially acceptable behavior while functioning as two-way ambassadors. They also hoped that the volunteers would accept the former patients as human beings, with some handicaps. This would show the community at large that former mental patients were people like everybody else, with fears and hopes, not monsters or dangerous people.

Working at the Friendship Center was a challenge but also fun and a source of great satisfaction. Unfortunately, there are only scattered remnants of that endeavor in the form of a consultation clinic and a day care center, the latter currently located at the former state hospital canteen—this over twenty years after its beginnings.

STEVE (JOHNNY) AND CAROLE, PLUS

S teve met his wife, Carole, at the University of Michigan at the Student Activity Building, when she was at a meeting about moving into a co-op house. In Steve's last year at the University of Michigan, he moved into an apartment at 807 North State Street. He took all sorts of household equipment to Ann Arbor, including an ironing board. He had learned to press his own pants and shirts, as well as cook for himself.

Henry and Ilse met Carole on Mother's Day 1961 and liked her right away. The next time they visited Steve, Carole's parents were also visiting, and they all got together. Later that year, Carole's parents and Carole invited Steve to accompany them to Florida during the Christmas vacation. The following summer Carole came to Traverse City to visit and meet the rest of the Adler family.

Steve was interviewed before graduation by several companies who wanted to hire young graduate engineers. While he was visiting Carole in Chicago, Al Goldstein, Carole's uncle, invited Steve to visit Motorola, where Al worked. As a result of this visit, Steve accepted a job offer from Motorola, where he worked throughout his career. He had acquired a degree in mathematical engineering, as well as in electrical engineering. He started to work in February 1962 and changed from a money-poor student to a well-paid employee of Motorola.

In April 1962, Henry and Ilse traveled to Chicago to celebrate Steve and Carole's engagement. They were married on August 18, 1962, in Chicago, where Carole had grown up. The wedding was a grand affair, with Bob as best man and Lil as matron of honor. Lil had been married the previous year.

Steve and Carole went to Denver and Seattle for their honeymoon. They had an apartment in Skokie, Illinois, where Henry and Ilse visited several times.

On the occasion of their first visit after the wedding, Steve wanted to take Henry and Ilse out to dinner—his treat. However, he made the "mistake" of also inviting Carole's parents. Maurice, Carole's father, stole Steve's thunder by sneaking into the kitchen and paying the bill. Maurice liked to play this kind of practical joke.

In 1964, Steve and Carole went on a trip to Europe. When they were in Vienna, they went to see the hospital where Steve was born, as well as the homes of Henry's and Ilse's parents.

For Thanksgiving that year, 1964, they invited Henry and Ilse to Skokie. They brought along Shelley, their niece. On the way to Chicago, Henry and Ilse picked up Bob in East Lansing. Bob was a student at Michigan State University then. On the way home, they encountered a severe blizzard and had a difficult time getting home.

The next year, on December 24, 1965, Darin Benjamin Adler was born. Ilse was stunned when Carole put him on her lap. He seemed a complete repetition of his father at that age. Ilse just sat there and gazed at this wonder—a typical grandmother.

Henry and Ilse visited back and forth frequently between Skokie and Traverse City. On Thanksgiving 1966, everyone was invited to Lil and Dan's in Cincinnati. Darin was already toddling, while Mark was still crawling. Maurice and Mollie, Carole's parents, also came. Maurice was a crazy shutterbug who always carried his heavy photographic equipment. It included a portable spotlight that had already produced in Darin an instant smile, a conditioned response to the light. This gave a lot to laugh about. When they brought Darin into Lil's bedroom, under a bright lamp over her bed, Darin immediately put on his smile for a photograph.

In 1966, Henry and Ilse wanted to avoid driving and flew to Cincinnati. In Cincinnati, Ilse wanted to reconfirm their return trip. The airline agent told Ilse that Henry's return ticket reservation had been canceled because he never got there. Ilse had to do a lot of persuading and finally had a reservation for him as far as Chicago, but to Traverse City they were on stand-by. In Chicago, there was plenty of room on the plane. Once they were on board they just sat there. Finally, after about half an hour, the stewardess spoke on the intercom and informed them that the pilot had been called away due to a family emergency. She said that they had to wait for a substitute and that the weather up North was bad. When they were in the air over Traverse City, the pilot tried to land three times. They could not land at the airport due to heavy cloud cover. The pilot informed them that he was going to Sault Ste. Marie, where they would be put up in motels and flown back to Traverse City in the morning.

In Sault Ste. Marie, Ilse called her sister, Susie, and asked her to tell the people at the hospital about the delay. In the morning, they again flew to Traverse City and again couldn't land. This time they flew to Grand Rapids. There was a heavy blizzard in progress, so the seventeen passengers who wanted to get to Traverse City unanimously accepted the alternative of taking the bus. They were taken by taxi to the bus depot. When they arrived in Traverse City, they attempted to get a taxi to the airport. A taxi driver informed them that no flights were operating due to the blizzard. They explained that they needed to retrieve their cars at the airport. When they got near the airport, the coast guard provided a snowplow to get into the airport and find their cars. So much for avoiding traveling in a blizzard!

Steve's second son, Mitchell, was born on April 3, 1968, shortly after Steve and Carole moved into their home in Highland Park, Illinois. Henry and Ilse had been on their way to Florida but came back to Highland Park, as Carole was ill and had to be hospitalized. Henry and Ilse wanted to help Steve with the children and the household. They helped Steve and Mrs. Henderson, who was assisting in Mitchell's newborn care.

During that year, 1968, Steve was completing studies for his master's degree in business administration. In September, at the occasion of his graduation, Carole (who was fully recovered) gave him a big party. Henry and Ilse drove to Chicago for the party.

Henry and Ilse visited back and forth through the years between Chicago and Traverse City. During the summers, the children and grandchildren came to Traverse City. In addition, during these years they established the tradition of spending Thanksgiving as a family reunion, taking turns in each others' homes.

On July 28, 1970, Scott Joseph, the third Adler grandson, was born.

Steve continued to work for Motorola. As part of his work, he traveled a great deal, which allowed him to occasionally visit Henry and Ilse during business trips.

LIL AND DAN, PLUS

L il and Dan were married on May 20, 1961, in Cincinnati. Henry, Bob, and Ilse went to the wedding.

Ilse was opposed to this interfaith marriage. As a matter of fact, Ilse was heartbroken. Until then, she had been unable to tell their children about the tragedy of the Holocaust and the probable fate of her parents. At that time, her child marrying out of their faith felt like a betrayal. When her daughter had come to her office to tell about her decision to marry Daniel, Ilse had been unable to voice her concern or verbalize her objection or the reasons for it. Ilse refused to go to the wedding until the last minute.

Henry and Ilse were in Detroit, visiting close family friends, Dave and Judy Orzech, when Lil called and begged them to come to the wedding. Ilse gave in and rushed out to buy suitable clothes, and they went to the wedding. Little did Ilse know then what a gem Lil had found in Daniel and that Ilse never would have had a chance in a million years to find or handpick a better man. Henry and Ilse loved him and were glad he was part of the family.

Henry and Ilse visited back and forth with Lil and Dan. After five years, Lil had not been able to conceive, so they decided to adopt. On August 16, 1976, Mark came into the family. On March 6, 1969, Jody became their first granddaughter. Then, lo and behold, after thirteen years of marriage, Lil became pregnant. On August 16, 1974, Matthew, their first "home-grown" child was born.

BOB AND BETTY, PLUS

On June 24, 1967, Bob and Betty were married in Aspen, Colorado. Their marriage is a good and happy one. They do not have any children.

Bob and Betty have had and still have a variety of pets. Betty is exceptionally good with them. They returned to Michigan to manage a restaurant. In Michigan, they lived in Okemos for a while. Bob went back to school at MSU but quit after one term. Then, after a variety of jobs, they opened their own restaurant, the Beggar's Banquet. Beggar's Banquet is still flourishing after over twenty-five years. Betty is artistic and very talented. She paints, and she has sewn all the patchwork tablecloths for the restaurant.

Bob and Betty bought an old farmhouse, with over six acres of land. They remodeled and enlarged this home, where they still live. Henry and Ilse visited back and forth a lot, as with the other children.

Several few years ago Bob and Betty took up sailing. They continued sailing until their boat sank, while docked during a rain storm.

GRANDCHILDREN

Darin and Diane were married on October 3, 1994.

They have a daughter, Sophia, and a son, Simon.

Mark and Brandy were married on April 24, 2008.

They have a son, Garrett, and a daughter, Alexis.

Scott married Christy Gunvalsen on October 5, 2005.

They have a daughter, Riley, and a son, Conrad.

Jody has a daughter, Arabella.

Matthew and Amiee were married on July 1, 2000.

They have a son, Aidan, and two daughters, Ava and Addison.

SOME FRIENDS,
RELATIVES, AND TRIPS

During the years Henry and Ilse lived at 223 Garfield, they had some very nice friends. Ben and Phyllis Fischer were artists who came to Traverse City from New York. Ben had a job at Burwoods Inc., designing pieces in their line of copperware. Ilse met Phyllis at a garden party, and they immediately took to each other. Phyllis invited Ilse to come to a meeting of the Women's Organization for Peace and Freedom. They became close friends. The whole Adler family had great times with them while they lived in Traverse City. They got together with them during Christmas 1947 at their log cabin near Suttons Bay. Phyllis had invited the family to come skiing on a nearby small hill. Later, when Phyllis wanted to drive them back into town, her car wouldn't not start. The Adlers got a ride home, crammed into the cab of a county snowplow. The family has several mementos from Ben and Phyllis—a set of silk-screen pictures of the peninsula landscapes and some copperware that Ben made.

They continued to keep in touch after Ben and Phyllis moved back to New York. Henry and Ilse visited them on a trip to New York in 1952. The last time Henry and Ilse saw Ben and Phyllis was in 1977, when they again visited them at their home in northern New York State. Henry and Ilse stayed with Phyllis and Ben during their last visit. This was at the Fischer home on Leatherhill Road near Pawling, New York. Their house was two hundred years old, and it was so interesting that Ilse had to describe it:

> As one entered the front door, there was a tiny hall. To the right was the living room, and to the left a large kitchen, which was used as a dining room and kitchen. In each of these rooms were big fireplaces, and the furnishings were partly produced by the Fischers themselves. Ben had a large loom in the kitchen. He had made a shaggy rug for the living room on it. Phyllis, who for the preceding ten years had worked as an arts and crafts instructor at the nearby Harlem Valley State Hospital, had made some samples of the things she had taught her clients, such as appliquéd throw pillows. Ben's handiwork was also in the kitchen. Ben had made countertops and splash boards inlaid with small tiles that he had made. Straight up from the entryway was a stairway to the upper floor. On both walls were great big designs also made with these tiny tiles [the stairway was not quite finished when they were there]. The upper floor contained bedrooms and a bathroom. In the guest bedroom, Ben had built narrow wooden beds. The rest of the bedrooms were furnished with antique furniture, dressers, and dressing tables with marble tops and ornate wood carving. In the back of the kitchen was Ben's workroom, where he did his pottery and metalwork. In addition, there were many pictures throughout the house, some of their own works and some from other artists.

Outside the house, Ben and Phyllis had a lovely flower garden. Also, there were flowering shrubs by the house and, a little further away, a vegetable garden. They kept the vegetable garden fenced in with a rather high fence to keep out deer and rabbits.

The plot on which their house stood had a gentle downward slope. They had a small in-ground swimming pool. Their neighborhood was sparsely populated. They showed Henry and Ilse that it was quite a distance to their next-door neighbors.

Just before Henry and Ilse left, Ben was in the process of making curtains for the dining part of the kitchen. Ben was using blue material with appliqués of half life-sized doves that he made. Ben was as handy with the sewing machine as he was with his artist's tools. Ben showed them some flannel shirts that he'd made for himself. Ilse said that they certainly looked like professional work.

Trips

In November 1939, Ilse took her first trip from Traverse City. She was pregnant and had started to bleed. She was afraid of a possible miscarriage. The doctor in Traverse City suggested that Ilse go to a clinic in Detroit, where Ilse had been examined before going to Traverse City. It was fortunate that Ilse and Henry's landlady, her sister, and their niece, Jenny Alper, were driving to Detroit, and they were willing to take Ilse along and bring her back. Ilse stayed in Detroit with her cousin Ellen (Ellie) Safier. Ilse went to the clinic, which was in nearby Oakland, Michigan. The doctor at the clinic asked her whether she wanted to keep this baby. Ilse told him yes, so he suggested that she go home, rest a lot, and not "go on any long car rides." During Ilse's stay at Ellie's, they went to see the new movie, *The Wizard of Oz*. Ilse's trip was at Thanksgiving, and Henry was invited to the Alpers'. Henry later told Ilse that he was appalled by the "waste of food" he witnessed at dinner because he was thinking about their family in Vienna who were starving.

After Ilse returned from Detroit, she asked the members of the Traverse City congregation for affidavits for the family in

Vienna. She was flatly turned down. After Susie came, Ilse tried to get affidavits in New York and Chicago, but she only got promises that were not fulfilled.

Ilse took her next trip to Chicago in the fall of 1940. This was another attempt to find affidavits for the family in Vienna. This trip was without success and again with empty promises. At that time Ilse was staying in Chicago with a couple from Vienna who had also tried in vain to get affidavits for their folks.

When Ilse was traveling back to Traverse City she ran out of money in Grand Rapids, Michigan. Jack Law, a friend who worked with Henry, drove Henry to Grand Rapids in his Model T convertible to pick up Ilse. It was cold and raining on the way back, and when they got home, Henry was very sick. Dr. Bushong came to their house and treated him with a new sulfa drug.

In 1945, Ilse went on a trip to New York, while a neighbor took care of their small children. Ilse stayed with a cousin in Brooklyn and tried to find a job in New York. Before Ilse started a job, Henry wrote, urging her to return home. Ilse returned by train. Henry and the children came to the train depot to pick her up. Even though Ilse did not earn any money to pay for this excursion she was glad to be back home. Ilse had the Adler home licensed for day care and earned some additional income taking care of that same neighbor's baby.

Ilse's next trip was in 1947. She went again to Chicago to meet her friend Hedda. Hedda was on her way to Washington, DC, to get help from the US State Department. Hedda wanted to get her mother out of Russia, where she had fled to escape the Nazis. Hedda succeeded, and her mother lived the rest of her life with her in San Francisco. On the way home to Traverse City, Ilse traveled with the Neimans. They paid her way on the train for helping with their three small children.

As described earlier, the whole family's first trip to Detroit was in 1949.

The next big Adler family trip was in 1952, while Ilse was between jobs. It was summer. There were no expressways yet, but there was part of the new Pennsylvania Turnpike, which began at Youngstown, Ohio. When they started out, they had packed a picnic basket. They were too poor to afford restaurants. They traveled as far as the Ohio/Pennsylvania border and stayed in a boarding house. There, they had two rooms for the magnificent price of nine dollars. The next morning they got into their car and drove as far as the entrance to the new turnpike. There, they splurged and ate a wonderful breakfast. Thus fortified, they continued their trip through the magnificent mountains and tunnels. It was summer, and the dogwood was in bloom.

Ilse got mad at Steve because instead of watching the scenery, he had his nose in a comic book. When they arrived in New York they went to their friends' the Fischers and stayed with them. They visited their relatives and friends and did a lot of sightseeing. They went up on the then-tallest building, the Empire State. They went to the Rockefeller Center to see the Rockettes and a movie. They also spent time in Central Park. The children went on their own by subway. They spent a lot of time at the Museum of Natural History and, according to Steve, the Hayden Planetarium. The whole family went to a Viennese restaurant as a special treat. Steve also remembers a Chinese restaurant in a basement on the west side, where everyone sat on cushions on the floor, surrounded by silken hangings. Just before they left New York, Henry was stopped for a minor traffic violation, and the police officer made him open the trunk to see if he had any dangerous contraband.

On the way home, they went by way of Niagara Falls. After a stop in a motel in Canada, Henry and Ilse had only ten dollars left. They then drove all the way home, which was a twenty-one-hour trip. Henry got sick. He had a cold and was exhausted.

Several trips after that were with the Wilcoxes to annual APA conventions, and they used those opportunities to do as much sightseeing as possible. Once, many years later, on the way home as they traveled through upper New York State, Ilse got lost during one of her driving portions. She studied the map when Henry took over and discovered that they were on the wrong side of the river, driving back toward New York City. It was only a forty-five-minute "detour." They were driving through such beautiful country that they were not too unhappy about the delay. It was spring in May. The trees and shrubs had fresh green sprouting, and the pussy willows were out. They drove along the Finger Lakes and onto the New York State Thruway. On the way, they stopped in Michigan at Bob and Betty's. It was an all-around satisfying trip.

In 1953, Ilse and Henry went to Chicago to meet George and Edith Roth at the Morrison Hotel. It was the Fourth of July. As they drove along the Outer Drive, they got into a lot of traffic congestion near Soldier Field. They were unaware of the festivities in progress. As Ilse stood at the hotel registration desk, someone leaned over to her. It was George Roth. Later, as they were sitting at breakfast, Henry and Ilse told them about their jobs at the state hospital. They both were working then as attendant nurses. George paused, looked from Henry to Ilse, and said, "I feel so safe." He always was such a wag. Henry and Ilse had a good but very short visit with them. The following year George and Edith Roth again came to the States. They had planned to come to Traverse City but had to cancel. Some of the equipment George was to repair took longer than expected. Naturally, Henry and Ilse were very disappointed.

Ilse's Nightmare Trip to New York

Ilse had another story about an "obstacle trip." In January 1960, Ilse's cousins George and Edith Roth came from New Zealand to attend a meeting at the United Nations in New York. They had told Henry and Ilse that two other cousins were also coming, so Ilse decided to join them.

Ilse was going to splurge and fly. When the date of her departure came, the Traverse City airport was iced in, and no planes could fly. Ilse the indomitable hitched a ride to Grand Rapids with her boss and two fellow workers. Ilse was hoping to get a flight from Grand Rapids. Nothing doing; no flights. So Ilse took a bus to Ann Arbor, where Steve was attending the University of Michigan. Steve lived in the Nakamura co-op house and had a car. Steve obligingly drove Ilse to Detroit's Metro Airport, where they again found all flights canceled. Back they went to Ann Arbor. Ilse had to find a room, since she could not stay at Nakamura House. When they called the airport in the morning there still were no flights. So Ilse decided to take the train. Ilse arrived in New York at seven o'clock in the morning and took a taxi to her friends' place on Eighty-First Street and Columbus Circle. On the way, the taxi lost a wheel! Luckily, there was no traffic, and nobody was hurt—only the cabbie's pride.

All the visiting went well, including a hair-raising, breakneck ride through Central Park at night—it was dangerous then. When Ilse was ready to leave New York on the train, her friend Phyllis Fischer got her a cab. Ilse never forgot that wild taxi ride to Pennsylvania Station through New York's rush hour traffic.

When the train arrived in Detroit, their friend David Orzech was there to pick her up. However, there was another calamity. Ilse's luggage was mixed up in a three-way switch. It took from eight that morning until noon to untangle it. Ilse was glad that the luggage switcheroo had been untangled since her daughter, Lillian, had borrowed the luggage from one of her friends.

The next morning David Orzech was to take Ilse to Willow Run Airport to finally fly home. He found that his car would not start. David ran two blocks to get her a taxi. The taxi driver practically flew downtown to the bus depot, but the bus to Willow Run Airport pulled out on the other side of the station as they arrived. Ilse was in tears and called Henry to tell him that she was taking the bus and why.

When Ilse arrived in Traverse City, the bus depot was closed, and there was no Henry! There was another lady on the bus who was being picked up by a taxi. Ilse asked that taxi driver to call her another cab. When Ilse arrived at home, she found that Henry had gone to pick her up. Henry soon came home. Ilse returned the borrowed luggage, and all was well.

More Trips

In 1972, Ilse and Henry went to Argentina and spent a month with Ilse's cousins. They arrived on January 29. They were told at the airport that Henry's luggage was mistakenly sent to Africa. The airport employees said they would bring it to them, which they did late that evening. After this experience, they learned to pack a change of underwear in their carry-on luggage.

That evening they had a family reunion party at the cousins' with whom they were staying. On the next day, they left Buenos Aires by car. They went with Ilse's cousin, his son, and the son's fiancée to join Inge, Ilse's cousins wife and Inge's maid. They had traveled ahead by bus the night before.

They rented a house together in a resort on the South Atlantic, called Los Acantilados. This was a small village. There was only one telephone in the local hotel. They were about five minutes from the beach. There were numerous small tentlike structures, called *carpas*, at the beach. These served as changing rooms as well as a refuge from the extremely hot sun. They reached the level of the carpas by a stairway from the street. They had to go down several more steps to get to the water.

The beach was supervised by two well-trained lifeguards who were effective in rescuing at least one person from drowning every day. Ilse could never figure out how they spotted people in trouble. Each of the guards carried a shrill little whistle. By the time they heard the whistle, the lifeguards were already in the water with a life ring or using a winch to pull near-drowning victims to safety. Each time this happened, the people on the beach applauded wildly.

Once, the lifeguards brought an unconscious woman near Ilse's carpa. The lifeguard proceeded to inject the woman with adrenaline. Ilse's cousin explained that the lifeguards were well trained, very well paid, and respected.

They witnessed another drama. Both lifeguards had to swim out to a person when the line from the winch broke. Someone screamed, "Helicopter!" One ran up the stairs to the street to the hotel to telephone for a helicopter. When the helicopter arrived, the three lifeguards and victim were already on land. Later that day, they talked to a lifeguard and Ilse took a snapshot of him.

They had another interesting experience in Acantilado at the beach. Ilse's cousins had left. It was Henry and Ilse's last day, and it was already late in the afternoon. Their next-door neighbor at the carpa excitedly pointed to the beach and exclaimed, "There is President Iamuzzi's daughter with her husband." Henry went down to the beach and asked the husband for permission to take some pictures. Permission was granted. Henry asked where her secret service agents were. She told him, "We don't need them in this country." Henry said, "If this were one of Nixon's daughters, the beach and the surrounding area would be crawling with police and the secret service. A simple citizen would not be able to even go near her." She laughed. She spoke perfect English and told them that she had worked as an airline stewardess before she married. Her husband was a well-known singer and TV actor. Later, Ilse's cousin told them that her father had been opposed to that match. The wedding had been televised and was a great national event.

They took some side trips with Ilse's cousins and saw a bit more of the country. At the end of their stay, they were in a hotel in downtown Buenos Aires.

In 1974 they went to Sao Paulo to visit an aunt, her son, her daughter, and their children. From there they went to Rio de Janeiro to attend the Carnival. After that, they went by boat to Buenos Aires, where they met their cousins and went to their home.

Later, they spent a couple of weeks in Mar del Plata, a large city on the South Atlantic coast. They were in an elegant hotel next to the largest casino in the world. They enjoyed this very much. They were able to walk a lot and saw many nice places.

In 1974, they went to Sao Paulo. They arrived at the airport, Viracopos, at two in the morning. The airport is about an hour's drive out of town. They were surprised to see Ilse's cousin, Lola's son, there waiting for them at the airport. He was the spitting image of his father.

He took them into Sao Paulo, a huge city with many skyscrapers and expressways. It took an hour to get to their hotel at the Praca de Republica in the heart of downtown Sao Paulo. During the next few days, they were taken around and visited all their relatives.

One day they were picked up by a chauffeured air-conditioned car and driven to Santos, Sao Paulo's harbor. This was where the original immigrants arrived. The expressway leading to it is called "Via de los Immigrantes." Sao Paulo is built on many hills, and the road to Santos winds down a mountain through many tunnels.

It was Carnival time, and Ilse's cousins provided them with tickets to the Carnival parade. They could only stay for two hours, but they saw two Escuelas da Samba. This is the name of the groups that prepare a full year for this event. Every entry chooses a theme and provides the lyrics, the music, the costumes, and the whole program for their entry. On several days before the big parade, the groups can be seen and heard all over the city of Rio de Janeiro.

In Rio, they stayed at the home of another cousin, who lived on the street that connected the Ipanema to the Copa Cabana. They went up on the Corcovado, where the fifteen-foot-high Christ statue stands. They also took the trip up on the Sugar Loaf Mountain. The views from both were enchanting. They felt that Rio de Janeiro was the most beautiful city in the world, at least that they had seen so far. When they were ready to leave for home, all the relatives came to see them off.

EPILOGUE

Henry and Ilse were able to spend many years together after retiring. They created a new extended family as well as making many new friends in the United States—their home and final resting place.

Henry died on November 13, 1997, at the age of ninety. Ilse died September 13, 2005, at the age of ninety-two.

The family reunion tradition Henry and Ilse began has been continued by their children, grandchildren, and great-grand-children. This is now the annual Adler/Ostendorf family reunion, held in the remodeled 822 Washington home. The Adler/Ostendorf family also sponsors films annually in their memory at the Traverse City Film Festival. Henry and Ilse's memory is also continued on the wall of the synagogue Beth El in Traverse City.

NOTES

Note 1

IX District (North)

60 Nussdorfer Strasse

Home of Ilse nee Goetz Adler; her father, Julius; and mother, Belcza (Bella) Goetz; and sister, Suzanne. Konditorei across the street. This is just north of the Franz Schubert Museum at 54 Nussdorfer Strasse.

Note 2

Suzanne (Susie) Fischman died Tuesday, July 19, 1994, at the Grand Traverse Medical Care Facility in Traverse City, Michigan, at the age of seventy-three.

Susie was born June 28, 1921, in Vienna, Austria. Susie was a former president of Temple Beth El and active as a volunteer in the Service with Love organization, Women's Resource Center, Grand Traverse Medical Care Facility, and Salvation Army. Her having survived the Holocaust in Europe and immigrating to the United States was featured in the Traverse City *Record Eagle*.

Susie's husband, Philip, died in 1984. Susie's daughter, Shelley, and Shelley's husband, Schaub, live in Newaygo, Michigan.

Shelley has two daughters, Jennifer Schaub and Rebecca (nee Schaub) Guyette. Susie also had a stepdaughter, Ruth Talamo (deceased) of Randolph, Massachusetts.

Note 3

XVI District (West)

51 Neulerchenfelder Strasse,

Home of Henry Adler; his mother, Jeanette (nee Austerlitz) Adler; his father, Sigmund Adler; and his brothers, Maximillian and Leopold.

Note 4

On May 21, 1935, Ilse Goetz and Henry Adler were married in Vienna, Austria, in the Central Synagogue, Seittenstettengasse 4.

Note 5

XXI District (East & North)

Brigittenau Hospital, where (Johann Stephan) John Steve Adler was born.

Note 6

Central Cemetery (Zentral Friedhof), Henry's mother, Jeanette Adler

1st Gate, Group 51, Row 18, Grave #39, Schreier family name

MISCELLANEOUS ADLER FAMILY AUSTRIA INFORMATION

Adler and Götz family Apartment

60 Nussdorfer Strasse, District IX, Vienna Austria

Three-story building—first floor: business establishments; second floor: building owner (Herr Bratman); third floor: Adler and Götz families. Five people occupied the apartment.

Rooms and Contents

There were five rooms and a foyer. There were three oriental rugs in the rooms. There were several paintings on the walls.

In the dining room were two china cabinets, one for dishes and the other shared space with books. One marble-topped buffet containing two Rosenthal fifteen-piece china sets, two china vases, one couch, a table, and dining chairs. A small table with a table radio. A baby grand piano. A violin.

In the child's room: A baby crib. A baby carriage. A bookcase and books. Two cherrywood wardrobes and clothes. A leather love seat that opened up as a sofa bed. A green marble false fireplace and mantel.

In the small hall and pantry: A window bench seat. A long mirror.

In the small room: Table and chairs and storage for personal effects.

In the bathroom and kitchen combination: A large tub, water heater, washboard, stove (gas-burning), cupboard for dishes, and an icebox with oak doors.

In the bedroom: Two blond cherrywood beds. A dresser. Two nightstands. A dressing vanity with three mirrors.

Personal effects

Baby clothing

A set of silverware

A silver serving set

A silver wine cup

A gold pocket watch

Adler and Götz (Goetz) Business Location

Wahringer Park, District XVIII, Vienna, Austria

Single-story building in the park, a coffeehouse and bridge (cards) club business establishment, owned and operated by the Adler and Götz (Goetz) families.

The location included areas for food storage and preparation, coffee making, baking, refrigeration for milk and butter products, and storage for other confections. There were inside and outside tables and chairs for customers. Several of the outdoor tables had umbrellas for rain and sun protection. Indoor and outdoor sheltered tables and chairs were used for bridge card games and bridge lessons for customers and students. Various social clubs also used the location for their monthly and bimonthly meetings

The business was open for most of the year, closing only during the coldest months from December through February.

Adler Family Business Location

Beyond the outer ring, Vienna, Austria

Two-story building at 51 Neulerchenfelder Strasse. A restaurant and inn business establishment, owned and operated by the Sigmund Adler family (grandfather Sigmund and two uncles, Maximillian and Leopold).

Additional Property Information

The World Jewish Congress in New York City has information that lists the names of Jews who lived in Vienna and whose property was confiscated. Both grandfathers are listed with reference numbers in that material. They are:

Reference # 11090 Dr. Julius Goetz, born May 21, 1879

Reference # 24330 Sigmund Adler, born June 17, 1870

A LETTER FROM ILSE'S AND SUSIE'S PARENTS

who perished in the Holocaust, most likely in Auschwitz, in 1944. Translated from German to English by Ilse Adler and Susie Fischman.

The Letter

The story you are about to read is true. Names have not been changed; no individuals need to be protected because most of them are dead. This is the remnant of the story of our parents, whom we left behind when we immigrated to the USA in 1939. Until America's entrance into the war in 1941, we had been able to correspond with each other and had kept our hope alive toward reunion after the war. At war's end in 1945, when we failed to hear from them, we gave up hope. Then, in 1948, we received the following letter, written in diary form on sheets of toilet tissue by our mother during her imprisonment. After their prison sentence had been served and they were free, they lived in Budapest until an unknown date in 1944–45 when the Nazis overran Hungary. What happened further, how and where they met their end, is unknown. Before they were caught the second time, however, they gave the diary-letter to one of our cousins. She and her family fled when the Nazis came and returned after the end of the war to find their home ransacked and plundered. An old rickety little table was left, and in its drawer was this letter, which the cousin then sent to us. The following is a translation from the German language. (It took twenty-one years to complete it, so great was our pain each time we tried.)

114

Budapest, March 29, 1944

My Father's Prayer

Beloved children—

Every day I pray approximately the following prayer:

Great God, there Thou art above the suns, above the stars, there Thou art everywhere and also where our beloved grand-children, where our beloved children are, where my beloved wife is, and there Thou art with me: Answer our prayers, give us the grace, unite us in life, health, freedom, love, happiness, and contentment. Let assaults and all plans of all our enemies become naught, everywhere and everyplace. Amen.

God bless you, my beloved, your loving father

Budapest, May 27, 1943

The Letter

My beloved dear children:

My heart will not give up hope that we shall see each other again in happiness, and that we, my beloved children, will be able to yet tell you all this with joy, and in person. However, in the event that cruel fate might not permit us to come to you, I am writing this all down, as far as I can remember, so that you at least might know everything, from the time on when we no longer were able to write to each other.

The last letter we received from you was from October 1941, and we still received it after war had been declared (by America) and we still wrote to you in December [1941].

Purely on the surface, at that time, nothing had changed for us. We still had our fixed income, in contrast to the unfortunates who had to exist from the breadlines and donations. We still had—in our own flat—the use of two rooms and the bath for ourselves, whereas most others had to exist four and five crowded into a terrible room. We always had enough to eat; truly good kind friends, among them also those downstairs in the house, faithfully supplied us with all we needed. So well, in fact, that we often, almost daily, could afford to have a guest for the noon meal. There were Lotti, Helen, Cilly, Mrs. Schmetterling, and once week also one of your father's poor friends to supper. When your father had to go shovel snow he also brought several hungry, freezing, and exhausted people who lived too far to be able to go home for lunch. We were always supplied with sufficient fuel, so that we were able to always have heat—even to the tune of a bath twice a week, with enough left over to help out a few of our friends with coal and coke. Others had to wait until the end of March before they were able to get a bit of fuel. We almost always had some guests who were glad to be able to warm themselves a bit. In that terrible time all stuck together more closely; the shared great suffering brought all closer. We got along well with our tenants. As a matter of fact, we got long exceedingly well, while many of the others, forced to live crowded together, on top of it all quarreled, thus making their desperate lives yet harder to bear.

Every Tuesday we had company. The guests came for conversational English. They at least felt comfortable for these few hours with us, as far as one could feel comfortable at all at that time. Our dear new friend Anny Weiss came always to these gatherings, and we learned to really like her—she proved to be a true friend in that difficult period. Mrs. Knoll and her brother-in-law came (her husband had committed suicide in the summer already). Then there came Lotti, Mrs. Schmetterling, Liesel there came Lotti, Mrs. Schmetterling, Liesel, Liesel Stein and her husband; occasionally Mrs. Kolban, Mrs. Shapira, so that at times we were ten to twelve people. We had plenty to keep us busy—we learned English, cleaned house, and straightened everything up nicely, washed everything up nicely, washed our laundry together, cooked together. Mornings Papa always went marketing and took Csibi-Darling (the dog) along, and every afternoon we went for a walk. We also still had sufficient clothes, shoes, and underwear, and we even had been able to shop for few things for our much-hoped-for and dreamed-of trip to you, my beloved children.

Thus, as I said before, superficially, things were still bearable, but inside, we were just as finished as all the others. As long as there was left even glimmer of hope to yet get out still bearable, but inside, we were just as finished as all the others. As long as there was left even a glimmer of hope to yet get out, one was able to hang on, but with the declaration of war, when all hope was lost to get to you, we were completely broken. All around us the despair, the many suicides. In that time the poor wretches, uncle Uncle Jacob, Gisa, and Alice jointly committed suicide. Poor Anny committed suicide. Poor Uncle Arnold, just had to go away; Louise and Schani were already gone (deported), and we never heard from them anymore, thus could no longer send them anything nor write to them. Unceasingly the transport went to Poland; often [the people of] whole houses, streets and districts were taken at once. We lived in uninterrupted terror and fright, and no more legal way to escape.

During the time, your poor father lost so much weight and became so thin that this definitely made me make up my mind, for his sake, to undertake any hardship and not to be a hindrance to him in any way, come what may. Now the only salvation was to get out illegally, either to Italy or to Hungary.

Of course, we first thought of Meran and began to investigate. You can imagine that then everybody everywhere had this in mind, and one really did no longer speak of any other topic. With lots of money, it was even then still possible to get to Switzerland, but many who had the money no longer had the courage to go. One heard much that was bad, how guides robbed the poor wretches and left them stranded. Also, that many suffered frozen hands and feet. It was deep winter then. Thus, much was discouraging. It was a difficult and real problem. For us it was even harder yet. We, although we had the courage and the determination, did not know anyone, and we had no money. However, in spite of this we did not rest. We were a group of people, among them also the Steins, who wanted most to go to Italy, but it was winter and the roads all snowed in over the mountains, and the other possibility with lot of money, naturally totally useless for us.

Now, Papa, shopping, had met a Hungarian, and since she also learned English, he invited her to our Tuesday Conversational English Hour. She mentioned, in passing, that she really could have gone to Hungary long ago, that she had many friends there who had been taken over the border by a dependable guide she knew, and that he also had taken one of her relatives safely across. Since Italy was so completely out of reach then, it seemed to us like hint of fate to have learned thusly of a dependable and honest guide, thus we decided to go to Hungary. We had no more time to wait. The deportations had again commenced at an increased tempo; night and day people were hauled away, and they could come after us any minute.

It is hard to describe now, how we sold the few things we still had, the everlasting packing and repacking; we had to be constantly ready for Poland, then again for flight, because it had been agreed that we must be ready at a moment's notice to go with our guide. This tension and constant worry and anxiety—even now that I am putting this down on paper, every single nerve in me jangles. And in that time we experienced the great joy of real selfless help from a few good friends. Everything had to be done in complete secrecy, not even our tenants must get an inkling of our plans. We wanted to take Lotti along, but she was too scared to go, could not make up her mind. Finally the day arrived when "Joscibacsi"—and to this day we do not know the man's real name—came to pick us up. At 6:00 p.m. we left our flat, accompanied only by our friend Anny, who however only came down to the house entrance, where she then stayed with Csibi-Darling. I still can see her, waving to us into the streetcar. She had the task to go back to the flat and tell our tenants that we might not spend the night at home. Everything had to be so arranged that in case of something going wrong we would not be found out. Now, with the streetcar, still with the yellow star on [our persons] up to the subway, where in the station restroom we hastily ripped off the yellow stars, then by subway to a prearranged stop where Grete's husband waited with our knapsack. We continued minus the yellow stars, but in fear of being recognized because we no longer were permitted to use public transportation, and if somebody would recognize us and report us, it would mean Poland for sure. We continued with streetcar No. 18 to the Meidling depot, where Joscibacsi waited for us on the outside. The waiting at the station—I wore head scarf and glasses and Papa wore his—then the trip on the train, again trembling for fear of meeting someone who would recognize us, but all went well, and at about 9:00 p.m. we arrived at the station from where we then had to continue on foot, and it started to get pretty rough then.

It was drizzly, clouded over, and windy. First of all, we had to get away from the station as fast as possible. The way was across wet fields, still soggy from snow. Our guide, very nervously constantly drove us—Papa with the heavy knapsack—all our earthly possessions; me with a briefcase and my purse. The anxiety, the darkness, the nervous Joscibacsi, and the horrible road—it was frightful. Suddenly I got stuck in the mud with one foot and could not go on. Joscibacsi swore, and threatened to leave me behind; finally with everybody's help I was able to free my foot, but the shoe stuck. By the time I was finally ready again to continue, you can imagine how it was to run on with the wet muddy shoe. Then came a long stretch along the slanting train trestle, always chased, always sinking into the wet snow, and so it went for over two hours, when we finally could slip close to a haystack, and Joscibacsi permitted a brief rest. We flattened ourselves against the haystack and ate a bite. The first stage had been reached. But half an hour later he started again to drive us on, still as fast as possible. Right across the fields and the vineyards, always away from the roads so that no patrol should grab us. We were allowed to talk only in very low voice and often had to proceed stooping low. Then we came near a village. We heard the dogs bark. Now we had to circle around the village, often we had to pass certain spots one at a time, and always listening and always alert to any steps [nearby]. Papa with his heavy rucksack and I ever so often thought that I could not keep up. And yet, how much more we had to go through yet! But always the one thought that kept us going and kept us on our feet: for our dearest, beloved children! We must—and thus we continued on. It was already around midnight when we finally came to a woods where our path had a bit more cover. But here there were at times places where we could hardly get through, the thick undergrowth, and then the dry leaves crackled, and we had to watch our step more and more carefully. Naturally, here too, we had to avoid the real path, because here it always was dangerous. We were still not at the border and had to hurry, but finally, finally there we were out of the woods. Here now, was the broad ribbon of a highway and across—finally—Hungary! We gazed across as if it were the Promised Land. Now we had to be twice as careful. This was the most dangerous spot. The moon was out and therefore that much greater danger to be discovered and perhaps get shot from both sides. Thus we had to run, one at a time, quite bent over, across the clearing, as fast as we could. Joscibacsi went first, then I, and then finally Papa and at last we were across.

We would have liked to throw ourselves down and kiss the ground; we thought were already safe, but very soon came the big disappointment: Above all we had to get out of this danger zone near the border as fast as possible, thus we ran a good way further into the woods. But this was not as dense and much nicer, and finally we were permitted to rest a bit again at a nice place. Though dead tired we were already happier and calmer. During this resting we discovered that we still had the yellow stars on our pockets, and we buried them in the ground, then and there. I think I could find the place any time; I can see it so before my eyes. When we started up again, it was already after 1:00 a.m. Now we did not have to hurry so anymore. We were supposed to get to Sopron not earlier than 4:00 a.m., where we supposedly were to be expected. There was now a long clearing in the woods and the path no longer so terribly hard. I, of course, was already very, very tired, but the gladness to be across the border buoyed us up. Never in all my life will I forget this road. One could see the road far ahead, and the moon was shining. Dear Papa and I held hands as we walked on, and when I seemed to be on the verge of fainting, we looked at each other, and "Ilse, Susie, Johnny, Henry, Lilly," etc. and we could go on. This alone, the thought of you, my dear beloved children, this alone kept us going at that time; And at that time we vowed to each other to hang on as long as our strength would last, not to despair and to keep on going.

Even so, we both almost very quickly despaired; as we talked, we walked out of the woods into the vineyards, and again halted for a brief rest at a small hut. We still had to keep very still and speak only in lowest tones: occasionally we heard someone whistle, and then we froze for fear that a patrol might be nearby.

Joscibacsi had given us tips on how to conduct ourselves when we entered the city, because if recognized as fugitives we would simply be sent back and that we feared as the most terrible thing. Therefore, he had called in a relative of his to carry our knapsack and luggage, and we were supposed to clean the mud off our shoes and all traces of the trek through the woods from our clothes; this also was the reason why we were to reach the city near daybreak when other people would be already on the streets. Thus it got to be three a.m., and we saw the city of Sopron. It was quite an unusual sight for us to see a city all lit up. At about 7 o'clock we were to be at the point where the man was to meet us. The plan was for us to continue by train [presumably to Budapest] as soon as we had recuperated from the trek on foot, because the sooner one could get further way from the border, the better. So, after again being warned to be very careful in the city, and especially keep out of sight of police or Gendarmes, and to try to disappear into a house, but in any event, I was to speak only Hungarian, if in anybody's earshot, but better yet not to be noticed at all. Thus we started, our guides went ahead; it was pitch dark, it was just my birthday [3/28/43]. As we rose, I could hardly get up on my feet and was in terrible pain when I started to walk. Papa had to lead me, and we made only very slow headway. After walking like this for a brief while we noticed suddenly that our guides were longer in sight; we started to hurry but in vain. We had just come to a crossing and had no idea which way to go. We waited a while, thinking they would come back, looking for us. We did not dare to rest and were extremely frightened, in the dark and in an absolutely strange place. When no one came, we decided to go to the city, and figured if they missed us, they would surely be on the road to the city also. In despair and upset we went into the city, and [saw] no trace of our guides. Meanwhile, it had become lighter already; here and there people were walking, and there were lights everywhere. So, you can imagine, every time we heard steps we thought, "Here come our friends," and we started to run, but nothing, no trace. We kept going hither and yon; and then we spied a policeman from afar; we immediately turned around and went the other way, and we could hardly think or speak anymore. We were agreed on one thing though—before we would let ourselves be sent back, we'd rather die! This in spite of the promise we had made to each other, just a few hours earlier, to hang on as long as our strength would last, because then it all would have been in vain.

We forgot that we were tired, we forgot our despair, and at long last thought to try to find the [headquarters of the] Jewish Congregation, yet we did not dare to ask anyone. Then we remembered that Joscibacsi had mentioned the name of the party where we were headed, but we could not quite remember it for sure. We wanted to call on the telephone, but we had no Hungarian money. Finally we went into a telephone booth and tried to find a similar name and the name of the street. Meanwhile, it was almost 6 a.m. and more people on the streets, so I took my heart in my hands and asked a woman how to get to that street. And we pulled ourselves together and went to that street but had to wait until the house entrance was unlocked because we had no money for the caretaker to tip him for opening the door. We had to get off the streets in a hurry because our clothes were mud-splattered and my stockings torn from the woods. Well, we went on upstairs and rang, half convinced to find our guides, when to our greatest surprise a very sleepy man in his pajamas opened the door and gaped at us, openmouthed. We begged him to let us in, [saying] that we were the party whom Joscibacsi had guided, etc. He let us in, and we found out that he was a total stranger who did know any Joscibacsi, etc. God helped us there and then, and we hope to God that this man will get his reward for what he did for us. He left us, went and fixed a bed for us, and made coffee and only after we were rested and had had some food and were refreshed did he ask us about all the details; then he telephoned a friend and the two of them then went to find Joscibacsi. You can imagine how we lay there exhausted. After two hours the two gentlemen returned, after finding Joscibacsi, who also had been running about, desperately looking for us.

Around noon we then continued our trip to Budapest, after again being fed by them and provided with Hungarian money for the train fare and having cleaned up our muddy clothes and shoes and provided us with some items from our luggage. All this had to be done without arousing anybody's curiosity, because it was strictly forbidden to aid fugitives. Everyone who got caught helping a refugee was himself severely punished and interned. This we had of course not known beforehand, [or] we would not have decided to come to Hungary. What then happened to us, you may be able to learn from others, because many here already knew about it.

Eventually we found a furnished room, but because we could not register by ourselves; we got into the wrong hands. In Vienna yet, we were told that eventually we could get legal papers permitting us to stay even though for a short time only, and such a temporary permit could be renewed, and that was we hoped to do. However, as mentioned, we got to the wrong parties, and it cost our last money to get some papers which actually only a regular citizen was permitted to carry. In the end we had a very nice room with kitchen and bathroom to share and even a balcony available, but then fate caught up with us. The man who had gotten us our papers was arrested and gave our names, and thus we were arrested on Whitsuntide Sunday of 1942.

It has been now over a year that we have been in prison, where I am now writing this. So far God has protected us and preserved our health, knock on wood. For the time being we are only in pre-sentence investigation and expect to have our hearing in the fall. After getting free we hope to get into a camp and there, with God's help, to wait out the war. What we have gone through here and how we are able to bear it all is not so easy to describe. Essentially we are being treated well. After two months, I already received food from the outside; dear Papa, however, not until after eight months. Up to now the physical part of it is bearable. Of course, we both were in the beginning quite brokenhearted and thought that we could not stand anymore. Especially when Papa was taken elsewhere,

I lost all composure and thought my heart would break. I never cursed anybody, but then when I was so completely separated from all those I loved, and found myself in prison, I did curse all, especially those who could have helped us so easily to be there with you and did not do it! May God reckon with them—he will [He did]. All the bitter tears that we cry from our aching hearts, so far from you, our beloved ones, may they sear their hearts! And you, too, must never, never forgive them! Since a few weeks ago Papa is back here in the same building, and I can at least see him from afar every Friday night at services. We both are very happy that now at least that much is given us. Dear Papa looks relatively good, and I myself look good, too. But we have aged a lot; we have become very old. My hair is quite gray and my eyes have suffered a lot. Well, may God now help us on. Our only prayer is to see you once again, my dearest beloved, and to be able to live with you, even if only on bread and water! Only this one should fate grant us, then we will gladly bear anything until then. In spirit I am with you always and with your darlings, and by imagining them I can bear life without you. If we only could have gotten any news from you. May God grant you a happy life in freedom. May you achieve what my mother's heart can beg from fate for you. My beloved dear children: I shall pray for you, wherever I may be. For your happiness and your life. I kiss and embrace you.

Your Mutti

Budapest, June 17, 1943

My dearest:

Today it is September 9, 1943. Here in prison we have heard of Italy's capitulation. We were supposed to have our hearing today, but it was postponed. Our hearts are full of hope! You can imagine how we feel. May God help us to hold out to the hopefully near end. I always carry this letter on my person; that is why I had to mark this day. We kiss you. We are well.

EPILOGUE

In the midst of heartbreak, horror, and terror, these two beloved people were able to cling to hope and to share the last little bit they had with their less fortunate fellow victims of persecution. The noblest evidence of compassion and man's *humanity* to man flows from their words, thus giving testimony to the everlasting truth and beauty of love and faith. No marble monument can do them greater honor, although we know no grave where we may mourn them.

THEIR DAUGHTERS, ILSE AND SUSIE

This book, *Our Story*, was begun several decades ago by Ilse Adler. The book focuses on the lives of Ilse and Henry, recounting their courtship, life together in Vienna, escaping the horror of the Third Reich takeover, and their subsequent life in the United States. The book has had several iterations as Ilse added life chapters over time. Much of the writing was facilitated by her introduction to computer word processing by her grandsons. Editing by (John) Steve Adler, her eldest son, was requested by Ilse during later stages of her writing. The editing was supplemented by several oral history tapes recorded at various Thanksgiving family gatherings. Later versions of the book were shared orally with Henry and other family members prior to Henry's passing in 1997. Henry and Ilse's children, (John) Steve, Lillian, and Bob (Robert) find that the book continues to stimulate their memories about their early lives in Traverse City and their wonder at the abilities of their parents to provide a rich and enduring family environment during difficult times in the 1940s and 1950s. As Bob's, Lil's, and Steve's lives move on, many related memories have arisen, but those are for another book at another time.

Henry and Ilse in the mid-1930s

The Adler family in the 1940s

CPSIA information can be obtained
at www.ICGtesting.com
Printed in the USA
LVOW07*0424080617
537304LV00004B/5/P